LAW SCHOOL SURVIVAL:

A Crash Course for Students by Students

BY GREG & SHANNON GOTTESMAN & FRIENDS

Macmillan Reference USA

A Simon & Schuster Macmillan Company
1633 Broadway
New York, NY 10019-6785

Macmillan Publishing books may be purchased for business or
sales promotional use. For information please write: Special
Markets Department, Macmillan Publishing USA, 1633 Broadway,
New York, NY 10019.

An ARCO Book

ARCO is a registered trademark of Simon & Schuster Inc.

MACMILLAN is a registered trademark of Macmillan, Inc.

Manufactured in the United States of America

10   9   8   7   6   5   4   3   2   1

Library of Congress Number: 98-84552

ISBN: 0-02-862296-0

Table of Contents

In memory of our Uncle Chester L. Brown.
He loved being a lawyer.

Acknowledgements

Although only two names appear on the cover, many law students helped us write this book. The contributing authors we asked to participate are all top law students and, more importantly, friends. The book is as much theirs as it is ours. These contributing authors (followed by the chapter they worked on) include Todd Kim, "Introduction to the First Year"; Neal A. Potischman, "Preparing for Class"; Jim Trilling, "Preparing for Exams"; Jodi Golinsky, "Tips for Taking Exams"; Kimo Peluso, "Law Reviews and Journals"; Richard Lobel, "Extracurricular Activities and Moot Court"; Dan Ralls, "Financial Aid"; Joanna Giorgio, "Working During Law School"; Paul Sweeney, "Interviewing"; Sarah Kotler, "Having a Social Life at Law School"; Melissa Morgan, "Living Arrangements"; and Martina Stewart, "The Minority Experience."

Justin Ingersoll and Michael McCormack, cartoonists-turned-law-students, deserve special thanks for their wonderful and witty cartoons that accompany each chapter.

We also would like to thank our families for their support and encouragement. Part of this past winter holiday was spent editing when it might otherwise have been spent with family. We especially want to thank in advance Gloria Gottesman and Mary Brown for their help in publicizing this book.

This book would never come to fruition without the diligent help of our editor at ARCO, Linda Bernbach.

Finally, on behalf of the contributing authors and ourselves, we want to thank friends, fellow students, and professors who shared their anecdotes, thoughts, ideas, and insights that directly and indirectly shaped this book.

by Greg and Shannon Gottesman

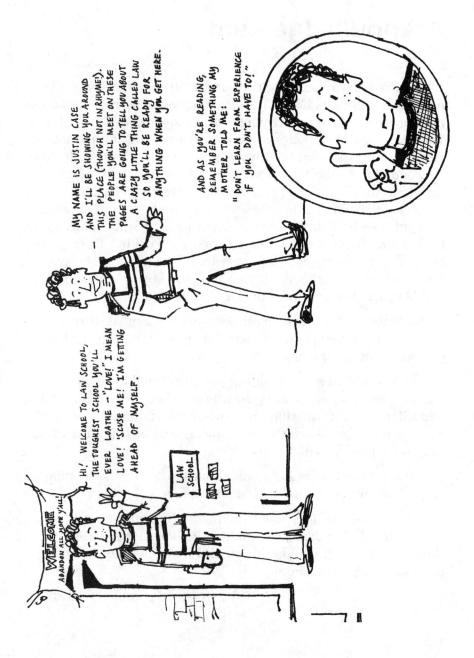

Foreword

The three years you spend at law school will be wonderful and terrible. Despite our efforts, this book is not "gospel." It does not offer a magic cure to the torture formally called the Socratic Method or a quick formula for learning the intricacies of Civil Procedure. But we are confident that this book will help guide you through what will undoubtedly be one of the most difficult and invigorating times of your life: the first year of law school.

Fifteen different law students contributed significantly to the content of this book; many more shared personal stories about their successes and failures. The information in this book is current. The authors and storytellers, with rare exception, are current law school students. They come from different schools and different backgrounds. We hope the following pages will be useful to every law student in some way. *Please do not read every page.* Skip around to the chapters and sections that most interest you.

Finally, remember that success in law school depends on one thing more than anything else: attitude. Law school is not easy, but it is not rocket science either. Keep perspective. Laugh whenever possible. And take time to smell the roses.

Good luck!

by Greg and Shannon Gottesman

CHAPTER 1

Introduction to the First Year

THOUGHTS ON THE FIRST DAY OF LAW SCHOOL

Sucker.

You sat there, laughing uneasily, while all your college "friends" made two hours' worth of lawyer jokes at your expense. (Q: What's the difference between a dead rat in the road and a dead lawyer in the road? A: There are skid marks in front of the rat.) You listened to your mother crying on the phone and told her that everything would be all right, that you wouldn't become like Them. You read *One-L.* (You know you did; you're not fooling anybody.) Yet despite all that, despite that warning blaring in your head—*Run! Run, fool, run!*—you're still here, ready to start your first class on the first day of what (there's no doubt in your mind) will be the worst year of your life. Yeah, that's right, you're going into your first year of law school.

Sucker.

Look to your left, look to your right: future money-grubbing Dershowitz clones on either side of you, right? Look at Them, sitting there all smug. They'd probably sue their own mothers if they had half a chance. (Q: Why won't sharks attack lawyers? A: Professional courtesy.) You don't belong here. This isn't for you; this is for somebody else. Isn't it? But what if you become like Them? Or worse, what if you already *are* like Them?

The urgent voice in your head begins to sound a little more reasonable—*Run! Run while you still can!* Your muscles tense as you crouch low in your seat, ready to explode into movement like a leopard who has just realized it doesn't want to be a lawyer. *Run, run, run!* Yes, in one swift and fluid motion, you'll be past the professor and out the door, romping free in the sunny, familiar world of non-lawyerdom. *Run!*

But you don't move. *Sucker.*

WHY SCOTT TUROW IS A WHINING NINNY AND OTHER INSIGHTS

At least, that's what you *could* be thinking on your first day of law school, especially if you read *One-L*, the book that, for some unfathomable reason, every law school applicant seems to read. Scott Turow wrote about the first year of law school as if it were a hell unimaginable, a period of such unending oppression that YOU WOULD BECOME ONE OF THEM, no matter how good your intentions at the beginning. There's something you should know about Turow's book, though: *One-L* is not how your law school experience will be. Read it as a fable and, more than that, as a fable written as if Aesop were a whining ninny. Believe us, it's not gonna be that bad.

Still, there's something important to learn from *One-L*—a moral, if you will. Even if Scott Turow's world once existed, and even if law schools today were like that world (they're not), the key to avoiding Scott Turow's experience is this: **Moral No. 1—Don't be a Scott Turow.** How well you do in law school, and how much you're able to enjoy it while you're there, depends on you. Sure, law school's not going to be all champagne and caviar, but it needn't be *One-Hell*, either. It's within your control, and this book is going to try to give you a little help in how best to exercise that control.

The most important thing to remember while reading this book and whenever you get advice about law school, though, is this:

Moral No. 2—Do what works for you. Try things out, figure out what works for you, and do that. You'll hear lots of methods, approaches, and systemologies, especially in your first year of law school. Some of these may turn out to be miracle cures; most will inevitably be miracle crap.

Do what works for you.

It sounds so common-sensical that it's stupid, but you'll be surprised to see how many of your classmates fall into meaningless routines and kill themselves with unnecessary, unhelpful work, work that will not help them do well in law school. It's so easy to follow a plan. It soothes your conscience to know that you did X and Y and Z before getting your three hours of sleep. It's nerd machismo: If you've done 15 hours of work under your plan, it means you've done three times as much as that slacker who's only done five. But, as some of your less enlightened classmates will be dismayed to find, three times as much work doesn't mean you'll get three times as much out of it, just that you worked 10 extra hours. (If it helps put things in perspective, quantify this time in terms of a currency you value: 10 fewer hours spent with your loved one(s); 20 fewer episodes of the *Simpsons* watched; 60 fewer beers drunk; a whole lot less sleep.)

We're not saying don't work hard; just don't work stupid. Yes, it's hard to evaluate and reevaluate your work habits to make sure they are efficient and effective. Yes, it's hard to be critical of your own study methods. But it's immensely important. Always be sure that your work is getting you somewhere; don't just work for the sake of working! Be alert: Repeating an empty ritual will feel good, and the repetition of the ritual will reinforce your sense of how important you think that ritual is. Keep your goals in mind and ask yourself if what you're doing is helping you get there. We're going to give you some advice that works for most people, but remember that nobody knows you better than you do (that is, of course, nobody except the FBI and that creepy 12-year-old who's profiled you on the Internet). The mantra one more time: *Do what works for you.* It's the best way to keep successful and sane in law school.

Now this leads to one more point: **Moral No. 3—Remember who you are.** Again, this sounds silly, but the rate at which law students lose themselves in the beginning makes the first year of law school seem like the Bermuda Triangle (except with more reading). Don't think that to do well in law school you have to change who you are, that you have to become some bland, tireless automaton; it won't necessarily work (see Moral No. 2, above). Keep your sense of humor about things. Step back every now and then. Are you becoming like Scott Turow (see Moral No. 1, above)? If so, be afraid. Be very afraid.

> *I was afraid. I spent my first day of law school looking around at all the other students who I thought were smarter than I was. I had read One-L by Scott Turow and thought my experience would be just as bad. I had heard the reading required in the first year was undoable. The classes were supposed to be harder than any I had taken in undergraduate. One person told me I could forget spending any time with friends or my wife. How ridiculous! The first year of law school was hard, but so was learning to ride a bike. I wish someone had given me the old FDR quote: The only thing you have to fear is fear itself. I spent more time worrying during my first year than actually studying. What a waste!*
>
> —Greg Gottesman, Harvard Law School

One thing that might help is this: Before you start law school, write down all the reasons you're going. Do you want to be a public defender or a prosecutor? Great. Do you want to save the environment from corporate greed? Wonderful. Is your goal to work for a law firm and make lots of money? That's fine, too. Your list of reasons for law school will serve as a beacon; when you feel lost, go back and read it to remind yourself why you're doing what you're doing. It sounds silly, but it's a whole lot better than waking up one morning and realizing that you hate where and who you are.

THE FIRST-YEAR COURSES

Okay, time to jump off the soapbox onto some brass tacks. (Ouch.) What can you expect from your first year in law school? You're a One-L, so you get very little choice in your courses, if any. Let's take a look at your course schedule and see what you've got: Civil Procedure, Constitutional Law, Contracts, Criminal Law and Criminal Procedure, Property, and Torts. (Your courses may differ slightly from those listed here. If so, we advise you to buy another copy of this book and hope that one has the same courses as you have. If necessary, repeat.) Toto, I don't think we're in college anymore.

CIVIL PROCEDURE

Despite its name, this course does not teach the rules of etiquette in civil society—far from it. You will not be learning where to put the shrimp fork and whether to bow lower to a colonel or a bishop; rather, you will be learning the rules by which civil litigation (that is, lawsuits other than criminal prosecutions) proceeds. Indeed, "Civil Procedure" is one of the least appropriate names in history for a course, because if there's one word that *doesn't* describe litigation, that word is "civil." The whole reason we need this course in the first place is because lawyers *can't* be civil: when the courts' desire to make litigation fair combines with the lawyers' incentive to wheedle, haggle, and connive every possible advantage out of the system, the result, as you'll find, is that rules can become quite complex.

In Civil Procedure (or, as it's commonly known, Civ Pro), you'll learn about the Federal Rules of Civil Procedure, which are the rules by which federal courts conduct civil litigation. (Most state courts have rules similar to the Federal Rules, and some law schools teach the rules specific to their states.) You will also read a number of cases from the United States Supreme Court that deal with some very basic and very important questions. For instance, who can be sued? When can you sue? Where can you sue? What techniques can you use to discover evidence in your case? How and when can a court dispose of a case?

These questions sound simple, right? You say, "These questions do sound very simple. The answers must be too, right?" The professorial reply, "In law school, you will learn not to sound so foolish." You mutter under your breath, "Lousy smart-ass." Sorry to be so rough on you. This little dialogue is meant just to get you used to the idea that some of your professors may use the infamous Socratic Method, which in theory means they never tell you anything straight out, but instead try to elicit everything from the class by posing questions and leading an ongoing intellectual dialogue. Done well, the Socratic Method is nerve-wracking, unpleasant, and surprisingly effective; done poorly, it just means that the professor acts like an ass and makes you feel bad when you don't know the answer.

For some reason, a lot of the more traditionally Socratic professors teach Civ Pro; indeed, in a lot of ways, Civ Pro is the most law-school-ish of all your first-year classes. This is a very nuts-and-bolts class. There are rules. You learn them. You apply them. You explore various doctrines that can be surprisingly interesting and a lot of fun to say. You can wow your mother: "Mom, today I learned about offensive non-mutual collateral estoppel!" "That's nice, dear. And are you eating well?" "Yes, Mom." Yes, you will learn that normal people are not interested in offensive non-mutual collateral estoppel or Civil Procedure in general, but you're not a normal person anymore, are you? Taking Civ Pro is in a (*very* remote) way like losing your virginity: You can never go back to those bygone days of innocence.

> *Civil Procedure was my favorite class. I was probably the only one who thought that way. Civ Pro is about learning the rules and language of being a lawyer. And you can't really begin to think and act like a lawyer until you know what you can and can't do. That's Civil Procedure. There's no other first-year class like it.*
>
> —SHANNON GOTTESMAN, BOSTON COLLEGE LAW SCHOOL

CONSTITUTIONAL LAW

You know Con Law. You're excited about Con Law, no doubt, and rightly so. Con Law is a sexy class. You address big, capital-"I" Issues: abortion, affirmative action and racial discrimination, separation of church and state, gender equality, and freedom of speech. It's big, it's fast, it's fun. But we're getting ahead of ourselves; let's back up for a second.

The Constitution, of course, controls how the government can function. It sets up the three branches of government and says what each can and cannot do. There are affirmative grants of power—the president, for instance, is given the power to command the military—and there are negative prohibitions—Congress cannot, for instance, establish a national religion. There is the well-known—freedom of speech—and the obscure—the right to prevent militias from being quartered in your house (really, it's in the Third Amendment). There is the noble—the right to equal protection under the laws—and the contemptible—slaves valued at three-fifths of a person each.

So there's a lot there. And especially because no one, not even the Supreme Court, can agree on what all the words in the Constitution mean—or even by what interpretive method they should be read—there is a lot of debate and a lot of room for creativity in

Constitutional Law. Not surprisingly, then, there's also a lot of variety in how professors teach Con Law. Expect at least some basics, though: You will learn about freedom of speech, due process, equal protection, religion and the state, and what Congress is empowered to do. And, of course, you will read lots of opinions from the Supreme Court explaining, changing, and, in some cases, muddying the contours of Constitutional Law.

Here's something important you should know about Con Law, though (and something you should remember in your other classes): A lot of people care a lot about a lot of the issues in Con Law. You'd have to be living in a cave (or be a talk radio host) not to know, for instance, that abortion has reasonable people on each side of the issue who believe very passionately in their own correctness. One key to fostering a healthy first-year experience is to be sensitive (and to encourage others, gently, to do the same). Argue your position, yes, but remember that neither being a lawyer nor being a law student means that you have to be (or have an excuse to be) an argumentative ass as well. Your life at law school will be much more pleasant if all your classmates don't hate your guts.

But have fun! Get in there and have some vigorous (and respectful) debates. Con Law is very interesting. In truth, very few people actually go on to practice Con Law, but it's something every lawyer needs to know and every law student needs to take.

One side note: At some schools, Con Law is not taught in the first year, but is required in the second year. So, if you miss out on Con Law your first year, don't fret. You'll still get to read *Brown v. Board of Education*, just one year later.

CONTRACTS

The other ones probably looked at least a little bit fun to you, but Contracts? It doesn't seem quite the course you would have taken as an elective in college. Chin up, though! Contracts can actually be quite a bit of fun, and the right professor can make it a highly entertaining experience. Some very interesting and important theoretical questions—What makes a contract? When and why will we allow someone out of a contract? If somebody breaks a contract, what should the wronged party get in compensation?—allow for stimulating discussions on contract theory. (Bet you never thought you'd read "stimulating" in the same sentence as "contract theory," eh?)

Of course, there's a lot of unavoidably boring stuff, too. Most Contracts courses teach about the Uniform Commercial Code (the U.C.C.), which in most states (with slight variations) governs the sale of goods. Depending on your professor, you may have to learn every tiny detail of the dreaded U.C.C. (good luck, we'll pray for you), or you may just have to know that it exists.

Now there's something different about Contracts from the previous two classes. Civ Pro and Con Law are dominated by decisions from the Supreme Court. In Contracts, by contrast, you will read cases from all sorts of different courts around the country (and maybe even some from other countries, depending on how wacky your professor feels). You see, Contracts is a so-called "common law" class. Maybe you've heard of common law marriages? The term "common law" refers to judge-made law—that is, to the principles that judges, over many years, have developed incrementally, from decision to decision. Judges try to maintain consistency from precedent to precedent, so as courts make decisions dealing with certain issues, they establish common law rules. Basically, today the common law fills in the gaps where statutes and constitutions don't give the answers.

In Contracts, you read common law cases chosen by your professor to illustrate broad common law concepts—for instance, that a contractual promise is not considered binding before the law unless the promisee also agrees to do something for the promisor. As you read cases, you will see how the principles fit together in concrete factual situations. You'll learn amazing bargaining techniques that will help you in real life. Soon enough, you'll be negotiating multimillion-dollar contracts for Fortune 500 companies and Hollywood movie stars. The last two sentences are complete fabrications, but Contracts is still pretty fun.

CRIMINAL LAW AND CRIMINAL PROCEDURE

The glamorous side of the law! Homicides; *Miranda* rights; *Law & Order*; O.J., Kato, and Lance. In fact, Criminal Law is *so* glamorous that it's actually *two* classes: Substantive Criminal Law and Criminal Procedure. In some schools, the two are taught as separate courses, but in others, they are combined (too bad, you still only get credit for one class). Think of the separation this way: Substantive Criminal Law, which is generally referred to simply as Criminal Law, is whether what you did was a crime (and if so, what crime); Criminal Procedure is, generally, what the government can do to prove it. Or think of it this way while you watch *NYPD Blue*: Substantive Criminal Law dictates what evidence the police need to find, while Criminal Procedure lets you tick off which constitutional rights Detective Andy Sipowicz has violated on the way there.

Substantive Criminal Law, in turn, has two aspects of its own. The first is more theoretical in nature and asks about the various doctrines that run throughout Substantive Criminal Law. For instance, one important theme is that of intent and its various forms. In one formulation concerning the killing of another person, the four forms of intent are *purpose* (that you meant to kill somebody), *knowledge* (that even if you did not intend to kill someone, you knew it would be a necessary consequence of your actions), *recklessness* (that you knew your actions would have a high risk of causing somebody's death), and *negligence* (that you did not know of such a risk, but should have). The crime for which you can be convicted may depend on which level of intent you possessed. Other issues in Substantive Criminal Law include *causation* (when the law blames someone for something that was not a direct result of that person's actions) and *defenses* (things that will excuse you or mitigate a crime—for instance, the famed insanity defense).

The other main portion of Substantive Criminal Law is more catalogue-like in nature: the list of crimes—murder, manslaughter, rape, robbery, burglary, arson, and many others. Under the common law, each of these crimes has certain elements that the prosecution must prove in order to convict someone. For instance, battery is the unauthorized, intentional, harmful physical contact or offensive touching of another person. Each of these terms has some ambiguity at the edges. In Substantive Criminal Law, you learn about the basic elements and about the fuzzy areas. For instance, under the common law definition of battery, a punch certainly fits, but how about an unauthorized kiss? (Technically yes, although try convincing the district attorney to bring a prosecution.)

Criminal Procedure, by contrast, does not deal with what crime has been committed, but instead with what the government can do to prove it. Unlike Substantive Criminal Law, which is mainly driven by the common law, Criminal Procedure derives from cases by the Supreme Court interpreting the Constitution (and, in particular, the Fourth, Fifth, and Sixth Amendments). In Criminal Procedure, you learn about what types of searches and seizures the police can do; when and for what purposes criminal suspects are entitled to consult with counsel; and how a criminal investigation must proceed in order to be constitutional. (By the way, a good way to "study" Criminal Procedure is to watch cop shows and call out the constitutional violations as they go, but don't try to cite *Hill Street Blues* as a legal authority on your final.)

PROPERTY

Property is about ownership, which, as you'll soon find, is not such a simple concept. You learn about what kinds of property interests people can possess in both land and goods, about how they acquire those interests, and about how they can convey them.

Property, even more than the other courses, scares people. Perhaps that's not surprising; not only is it a common law class, but it's an *old* common law class. The cases and doctrines you learn in Property date way back—back so far that they come from Jolly Olde England many, many centuries ago. Unfortunately, property law has been constantly prodded and poked over the centuries to accommodate various historical trends. Now, it is a near-hopeless morass of outdated doctrines like the destructibility of contingent remainders, the rule from Shelley's Case, and, of course, the infamous Rule Against Perpetuities. (Don't ask; you'll learn soon enough.) Yes, they're ridiculous, but that's not the point: Every lawyer before you had to learn them, and you will, too. It's kind of like a hazing ritual, but with the doctrine of worthier title instead of tequila. Party down!

At the same time, a surprisingly high number of people really like property law. It's kind of like a big puzzle. They give you the rules, tell you the facts, and ask you, in the end, who owns the property. (Resist the urge to answer: who cares?)

TORTS

Ah, Torts! Finally, Torts! All this time, you've been waiting for . . . what in God's name is a #$?#*$& TORT? The other class names were at least *words*, you're thinking; "tort" sounds like a rude word (or a chocolate cake). Here's the first important rule, which you probably just learned: Jokes about the word "tort" are not funny. You should not hope to impress classmates with any material riffing on the word—that's buying yourself a one-way ticket to Camp Pariah.

A tort, loosely defined, is a common law wrong you can sue for that's not based directly on a contract or property rights. Thus, when you get punched in the nose, that's a tort. If you were paying attention before, you know that it's also the crime of battery; the distinction is that you, the one with the sore nose, sue the puncher for the tort in civil litigation (again, hope you were paying attention before), while the government (if it chooses) could prosecute the puncher for the crime of battery separately.

But torts encompass a much broader range of legal wrongs than punches in the nose. Fender bender? That's a tort. Suing someone maliciously and without legal basis? Also a tort. Deliberately printing falsehoods about someone in your local newspaper? Yep, tort. Spilling billions of gallons of oil on a precious nature reserve? Tort. Reneging on your contract to sing at the Metropolitan Opera House? Not a tort, but a claim in contract. (Paying attention?)

Much as in Substantive Criminal Law, Torts has an abstract theoretical side and a more pedantic listy side. There are a number of themes that run through Torts: intent, causation, standards of care, duty, and damages. There are also a number of specific torts whose definitions have already been established by the common law: libel and defamation, wrongful death, false imprisonment, and negligence. Of course, some wise guys might argue that subjecting students to law school is in itself tortious, but that's neither here nor there.

English as a Second Language: Learning Legalspeak

And that brings up something you're going to have to realize right now. The first year of law school is like stumbling into a linguistic asylum from which you can never escape: Lawyers have their own language, and it's a language that can be really annoying sometimes. Sometimes it's inevitable—when you mean "collateral estoppel," there's really no other good way of saying it. But lawyers are not immune to the common conceit among professionals of using jargon not because it's necessary, but because it makes them feel smart or, even worse, because they don't think about making what they say understandable. You're going to hear tidbits of infuriatingly useless legalspeak like "arguendo" and "inter alia." You're going to read words so incredibly antiquated that you can't even tell what part of speech they are—words like "herewith" and "wheretofore." You're going to find yourself saying—to your horror—unspeakably hackneyed cliches such as "That's neither here nor there"; "That cuts both ways"; and "I enjoy seeing how much Jell-O I can fit in my pockets."

The esoterica of the language of law will, frankly, be one of the main things slowing you down in the first year of law school. Reading some of the cases will take a long time as you look up every third word in the legal dictionary. Unfortunately, you'll just have to learn to understand legalspeak. Just try to avoid falling into the trap of using it when it's not necessary.

But enough introductions. The first year of law school is just one year, and you'll get through it. Let's get on to the rest of the book. We promise: It'll be here *and* there and everywhere in between. It'll cut this way and that, and hopefully some other ways we haven't thought of yet. Wheretofore we request that you proceed forthwith to the text hereunder. (That is, turn the page, Jack.)

—BY TODD KIM

CHAPTER 2

Preparing for Class

> *Whether you prepare for class is a lot like playing Russian roulette. With about 100 people in the room, the chances that you will get cold-called are slim. But if you do get cold-called and you're not prepared, the penalty is severe. Being humiliated in front of classmates is only one of your problems. A professor at Harvard has a reputation for being especially severe. During the first day a few years ago, he asked a student a series of questions. When the student could not answer one of his questions, the professor simply walked out, with a disgusted look, never to return that day. Everyone looked around, wondering what to do. That was the shortest class first year.*
>
> —Greg Gottesman, Harvard Law School

THE SOCRATIC METHOD

Every law student has heard at least one story about a stodgy professor skewering an unprepared student in front of the entire class. Although the Socratic Method is in many ways a vestige of the way that law schools used to be run, most law students will tell you that it is still alive and well, especially in the first-year

curriculum. The Socratic Method involves learning by questions and answers, rather than lecture. A professor will ask one (or sometimes many) student a series of questions to take the class through complicated material. The class learns not by hearing the professor recite a factual answer, but rather through the progression of the questions and responses. And when a professor decides to "hide the ball" for a while to make the students work, this simple progression can feel like one of those family road trips that never quite ends.

Few aspects of law school are more feared, even by the smartest and most-prepared students, than the "cold call"—the moment when you get placed on the hot seat and are asked to answer a seemingly endless flow of questions. Learning how to do your reading and "manage" yourself in class can help ease the stress associated with the inevitable cold call.

ATTACKING THE READING

GETTING THROUGH THE ASSIGNMENT

Law schools revolve around the casebook. Before classes start, you will be asked to purchase a number of fat textbooks, each more expensive than the next, filled with cases and commentaries. Although casebooks are organized under a variety of systems, there are some routine patterns. Generally, each section in a casebook will contain one or two "big" cases that are supposed to explain a specific principle of law. After the big case(s) comes a series of notes mentioning smaller cases and scholarly works that refine the general legal principle at issue. For instance, a Constitutional Law text may contain a lengthy excerpt from the unanimous Supreme Court opinion in *Brown v. Board of Education*—the decision that prohibited segregation in public schools—and then subsequent notes will discuss 10 cases that followed *Brown* to clarify the opinion's impact. A given night's reading for one class will normally contain only one or two big cases.

To attack the reading, you'll need a few tools: the casebook, a pen and paper or computer, and a good legal dictionary. Some One-Ls are reluctant to invest in a legal dictionary, assuming that they'll be able to figure out most terms based on context. If you have any hope of understanding the One-L year, however, you should save yourself some time and a great deal of grief and purchase a good dictionary (i.e., *Black's Legal Dictionary*) on your first day. Otherwise, you'll be left in a world of confusion attempting to discern the meaning of phrases such as "an action in assumpsit," "plaintiff demurred to the complaint," or "we think res ipsa loquitor." As mentioned in the last chapter, law is filled with a tremendous amount of arcane language, some Latin and some English. Even the words you think you know—for instance, "removal" or "service"—can take on special meanings in the legal context. Learning the language of the law is a slow process, but one that you will grasp more quickly if you spend the time initially.

Your first reading assignment will probably take you a long time, both because you're not familiar with reading cases and because every other sentence will require the use of the dictionary. Just try to stay focused, however, and know that your hard work in the first few weeks will soon start to pay dividends.

Each time you come across a word you do not understand, it's best to circle the word and write a definition in the margin of the casebook. Few things make a student look more prepared in class than a quick answer to a question such as "What is trover?" or "What did the judge mean when she said that the issue was *sui generis*?" Although some students do not want to write down definitions, you'll find that it helps in the long term both for class preparation and studying for exams.

After you learn to understand the language of a case, you can begin to try to figure out the legal principles at issue. Keep in mind for which class you are doing the reading. You will read differently for your various classes. In Civil Procedure, for instance, the professor is going to be less concerned with the substantive law than with the procedure of the case (who sued whom, how it got into this court, what is the source of jurisdiction). In Contracts, by contrast, the professor is more likely to focus on the nature of the agreement between the parties.

You then tackle the reading slowly. Casebook reading takes a lot more time than most books you read in college, and you'll probably find it hard to understand the material if you're also watching the *Simpsons* or listening to Bob Marley. After you've found some peace and quiet and opened your casebook, start by trying to figure out the "big picture" idea behind each case. In Property, the case may stand for the idea that a landlord cannot break a lease without a good reason. In Criminal Law, the case may decide that a murder conviction is only appropriate where the defendant intended to kill the victim. Regardless of the class or the assignment, there is normally at least one big idea in each reading assignment. That big idea is usually called the "general rule" or "rule" of the case(s).

A crucial skill that you will learn is to search for the "holding" of the case. The holding tends to be the most important portion of the court's opinion because it is where you learn definitively what the judges have decided. "Dicta," by contrast, is that portion of the opinion ultimately irrelevant to the result reached. A couple of examples may help clarify the distinction.

"Mr. Jones is clearly a good individual. When the bank teller accidentally gave him $1,000,000 rather than the $10 he intended to withdraw, he did what anybody else might have done—he purchased a large home for his family and a pony for his child. Nonetheless, we find that he had an obligation to return the money to the bank because he knew it was not his own."

Although the first two sentences are interesting and contain useful information, the court's holding is that Mr. Jones was obligated to return the money to the bank because he knew it did not belong to him.

"When Ms. Jones refused to testify at her trial for robbery, the

trial judge called her decision 'very suspicious' and told the jury that 'only a guilty person does not testify.' The judge appears to have forgotten that in our legal system, the accused need not testify on her own behalf and is presumed innocent. But Ms. Jones did not object to the judge's remarks in a timely fashion, and therefore waived her right to appeal on this issue."

Insofar as the comments about the judge's error in this case are irrelevant to the ultimate decision, they represent dicta. The holding of this case is that the accused waived her right to complain about the judge's comments by not objecting to them in a timely fashion.

It's important to understand the holding of every major case that you read. Class time is often spent testing the limits of a decision's holding and seeing how it might apply to a different set of facts. Ultimately, exams will also test this same skill by giving you a complicated set of facts different from any case that you have read. Professors want to see your ability to take a general rule from one case and apply it to another. The only way to succeed in this endeavor is to understand the rule that each case provides.

After you feel that you have grasped the big idea of each major case, you should turn to the remainder of the assignment, which will attempt to challenge the legal principle just announced. The notes following a big case will contain brief summaries of additional cases (often called "squibs") and articles, along with numerous questions designed to make you think about the reading. This reading tends to be more time-consuming than reading the big cases because the casebook is trying to make you think about a multitude of hypothetical situations. Although you will never be able to remember even half of the squibbed cases and articles, the material after the big cases sometimes contains very important information. After all, a big case in Property may tell you that a landlord must keep a building "safe," but it is the subsequent cases that actually define the term "safe."

BRIEFING CASES

In an effort to prepare for class and do the reading carefully, new law students should attempt to "brief" the major cases presented in the reading. Some students brief the cases throughout the One-L year; other students last only a few weeks. Briefing can be time-consuming, but learning to do it properly is a useful skill that can help both comprehension and anxiety about the cold call. You will have to decide for yourself whether briefing cases is a good use of your time. Below are a few tips to help you if you decide to brief cases, even if only for the first few weeks of class.

There is no single "correct" format for briefing a case, and different students will find their own templates. Generally, the idea is to reduce the case found in the book to a few short paragraphs that contain most of the relevant information. Even if you are not called on for a given case, you will find your briefs quite handy when you study for exams months later.

The easiest way to begin briefing is to type the case name at the top of a clean page along with the relevant court the case was decided in, the year of the case, and the casebook page on which the case starts—that will allow you to refer to the actual case should a professor call on you. You should then write a short paragraph detailing the important facts about the case for your own reference. It is important to remember that you will not be graded on your briefs and no one else need ever see them; they are simply handy reference tools to help jog your memory. So keep the factual summary short, and include just enough to remind you why the case is in court in the first place.

You should then write a one-sentence question about what you think is the major legal issue in the case (most cases have only one major issue). A good example from *Brown v. Board of Education:* Are "separate but equal" educational facilities inherently unequal? Next, devote a short paragraph to explain the court's holding and the rationale behind that holding. Remember that a professor is not looking for you to describe every facet of the court's opinion and essentially reread the decision to the class. Rather, the professor wants to hear what happened in a few short sentences. If the case has any dissents or concurrences, you should devote a sentence or two to each opinion. The most important aspect of these summaries is noting why the individual judge agreed or disagreed with the majority. If the opinion has been included in your casebook, it's likely that your professor will want to ask you which judge made the better argument and why. If you can figure out the general rule or big idea for a particular case, it is often helpful to jot that down as well, either at the top of the case brief or the bottom.

Case briefs range from 10 lines to more than a page. Keep in mind that the shorter your briefs, the more likely you are to continue doing them throughout the semester. Because making detailed briefs can be so time-consuming, many students give up on the practice altogether after only days or weeks in law school. Rather than setting an unrealistic goal of drafting a substantial brief for each case, you should consider jotting down short briefs after each assignment. At the end of the semester, it is far better to have briefed every case concisely than to have briefed a handful of cases with extraordinary specificity.

Below we have included a sample brief for *Pierson v. Post*, one of the most famous cases in property law. Again, the following brief is not the one and only "correct" brief, just one of many styles. Find your own briefing style, one that you can do quickly and one that helps you best prepare for classes and exams.

Sample Brief

Pierson v. Post, 2 Am. Dec. 264 (N.Y. 1805) (p. 10)

<u>Facts:</u> Post (plaintiff) is chasing a wild fox on uninhabited land. Pierson (defendant) knows that Post is pursuing the fox, but kills it anyway and carries it away. Post brings suit against Pierson for taking the fox.

Issue: Does the pursuit of a wild animal give the pursuer a right to that animal?

Holding: No. Capture is required.

Rationale: A wild animal is acquired by "occupancy" only. Pursuit does not confer "occupancy," although the mortal wounding of an animal does give possession to pursuer. Allowing possession based on pursuit alone would produce too many disputes.

Dissent: (Livingston, J.) Killing foxes is a public good. Thus, the decision should encourage killing these animals. Allowing wild animals to be acquired without capture best accomplishes this policy objective.

General Rule: Wild animals are possessed only when they are captured.

One additional word to the wise: Among the numerous study aids you will see when you arrive at law school are books of case briefs that correspond to your casebook. These books can be handy time-savers that help explain the more difficult material, but you should be wary of relying on them as a substitute for doing your reading. The first-year law school curriculum is designed to teach you how to think like a lawyer. Your exam at the end of the semester will not consist of questions such as "What happened in *Marbury v. Madison*?" but rather will require you to apply legal principles you have learned to a different set of facts. Although reading a commercial summary of *Romeo and Juliet* might have gotten you through your English Literature 101 class in college, reading commercially prepared case briefs instead of your assigned reading will not allow you to perform well on law school exams. There are few shortcuts in learning to think like a lawyer; commercially prepared case briefs are not one of them.

Handling the Cold Call

If you're fortunate enough to have a professor who assigns panels of students to answer questions for a given class day rather than randomly calling someone's name out of the blue, you'll likely have a comparatively stress-free experience. You'll do the reading, you'll be prepared on your panel day, and you'll swim right through the class. But because so many professors still insist on the virtues of the Socratic Method, it may be useful to know a little more about how to prepare for and handle the cold-call experience.

The Socratic Method is a notoriously nerve-wracking experience, but the practice of ruthlessly interrogating randomly chosen students may be falling into disfavor. Those professors who still use it have significantly lightened up on the severity of the questioning; one of my professors referred to himself at the beginning of the year as a "puppy dog." Sometimes even puppies can bite, however, and when this happens, one's classmates can come to the rescue. This professor had a student on the ropes with questions about an unusual case, one in which a defendant crashed her car into another vehicle while enraptured by religious visions. The woman saw a white light and believed that God was guiding her car and would help her fly like Batman if she pressed down on the gas pedal. Her lawyer raised an insanity defense to the tort claim brought by the victim.

The professor barraged the student with questions about whether we should dismiss a woman's conversation with God as "insanity." After a while, a quiet student in the back of the room slowly raised his hand. The surprised professor called on the second student. The student proceeded to note that we know that God wasn't really conversing with the defendant: Batman has no real super powers, least of all the ability to fly, and God, being omniscient, would certainly know that. The tension broke as the classroom erupted into laughter, and the professor moved on to another issue, to the relief of the initial student.

—Phillip M. Spector, Yale Law School

Case 1:   What to do if you're completely prepared.

This is, for obvious reasons, the best scenario. You've done the reading, the professor is going to ask you questions about the reading, and you're basically going to have a leisurely conversation that just happens to be in front of many other people. You want to stay relaxed, speak slowly, and listen to the questions carefully. Keep in mind that not every question is going to be easy. After all, there's a reason that your professor is the professor and you're a student. Be prepared to stop and think, be willing to admit that you do not know an answer, and be open to the idea that there's more to the problem than you first thought.

You should also remember that while you'll leave the professor at the end of the class, you're going to be spending three years with the students you see around you. There are few things that other students like less than arrogant know-it-alls. Answer the professor's questions and make any arguments you like, but keep in mind that you'll win few friends by making lengthy speeches or by quoting extensively from your college thesis. You should be thankful that you carefully prepared that day without feeling the need to prove how much you know about the law. Your professor will be pleased with your preparation, and your classmates will be pleased with your personality.

Case 2: What to do if you're partially prepared.

This can be among the more harrowing in-class experiences, because you do not want to go down in the professor's book as having skipped all the work, but you also do not want to get in too deep before having to concede that you are not prepared. Most students' experiences probably fall somewhere in this category. Although you did the reading, you certainly would have done it more closely if you had known you would be cold-called. Welcome to the daily dilemma caused by the Socratic Method.

The key way to handle partial preparation is simple: Make sure you are aware of what you know and what you don't. Answer any questions that you can from the material you studied, but be willing to admit your lack of preparation when the professor enters an area that you have not reached. Students say things such as, "I'm sorry, I did not get to that case," or, "I'm sorry, I only read as far as X." Resist the temptation to justify yourself with tales of being snowed in at the airport or personal problems with a spouse or significant other. You can deploy such excuses on the off chance that you get called to the professor's office to explain yourself.

Partial preparation is not the same as no preparation, however, and don't concede defeat before the first question is asked—after all, people are rarely as prepared as they would like to be. You may be surprised to realize how much of the reading you understand, and it is possible that you are dealing with particularly hard material that the professor does not expect you to have mastered. Thus, while you should be honest if the professor begins asking questions about reading you never reached, if you've made an effort at the assignment, do not be embarrassed to speak up.

One final note: Listen to the professor's questions very carefully. Even if you have not done all the reading, you may be able to answer general questions, particularly if they do not focus on the specific facts or holdings of cases you have not read.

I was cold-called just once in my whole time in law school. It was in Criminal Law, my first year. It was an awful moment for me. I stuttered, had no idea how to answer the question, asked the professor to repeat it, forgot what page we were on, missed the important point, forgot the facts of the case, and so on—basically your worst nightmare. I promised myself it would never happen again, and it never did.

Here's why. I learned an important survival skill for law school: the preemptive strike. The preemptive strike isn't really a thing; it's a mind-set, a way of life. It comes in all shapes and sizes, too. But all preemptive strikes share the same goal: to say something smart (or seemingly so) on your own terms, so when it comes time to answer the hard questions, you can cower in the corner and not get called on.

All preemptive strikes also share at least two common characteristics, which you must learn if you are to perfect the maneuver. First, preemptive strikes must be disguised as innocent insights or questions. If the professor sees through you (they usually do), your effort is wasted—or worse, you could be seen as a troublemaker. Thus, the preemptive strike must be good—usually an educated question, or a theoretical comment—but it can't be too good, lest you take the chance of having the professor so taken with you that you are "on call" throughout class.

Second, for your preemptive strike to be effective, you have to be remembered. Nah, the professor doesn't have to learn your name—that could be

> *dangerous, because she could end up thinking you are smart and call on you all the time. You don't even have to be checked off on the professor's (often nonexistent) list. All you have to do is give her the vague feeling that you've spoken recently (if you're really good, this feeling will stay with your prof for months), and baby, you are off the hook!*
>
> —JOSEPH K. LEAHY, NEW YORK UNIVERSITY SCHOOL OF LAW

Case 3: What to do if you're not prepared.

Professors have different policies for students who are unprepared. Some simply ask that you provide them with a note before class if you were unable to do the assignment. Others assume that if you are in class, you have done the reading. If you have a professor with a zero-tolerance policy, you might be advised to sit in the back on the days when you are unprepared so that your seat remains empty (called "back-benching"). If your professor simply requests notification before class on those days when you are unprepared, taking him or her up on the offer is advised. For there is nothing quite so frightening as being cold-called when you simply never cracked open the book.

The solution to this problem is in fact rather simple, albeit painful. If you are cold-called on a day when you are completely unprepared, you must bite the bullet and say, "I'm sorry, I'm unprepared." If you actually seem contrite and can avoid falling into nervous laughter— laughter that could be interpreted as your feeling that this whole matter is one big joke—you may escape with only a mild case of embarrassment. At all costs, refrain from offering up an excuse in front of the entire class. If you have a legitimate one, you may be wise to mention it to the professor on your own time. But at that moment, the professor is probably not in the mood to hear it.

Once you have been caught unprepared, you will likely have to spend the remainder of the semester dealing with the repercussions of your lapse by doing the reading carefully every day. Older professors have been known to conclude each class by informing a previously unprepared student to be ready tomorrow—yet when tomorrow comes, the professor does not call on the student and instead repeats the same warning for the next class. Such tactics keep that student in a sort of purgatory for the duration of the class as he or she never knows if the next day will be "the day." The best way to avoid this particular problem is to do your reading each night, even if you cannot always do it closely.

MAKING THE MOST OF CLASS TIME

TAKING NOTES

Thanks to the proliferation of laptops, law school students are now able to take down nearly every word of their classroom discussions on the computer. Although many students still take handwritten notes, either because they prefer a pen and paper or because a given professor refuses to let laptops into the classroom, laptops have come on the law school scene with a vengeance and show little chance of disappearing. Regardless of how you choose to take notes, keep these few ideas in mind.

I was totally excited by the law school phenomenon of taking notes on a laptop computer. Not only could I type five times faster than I could write, I loved the idea of being easily able to pull up my case briefs for reference during class. So the first thing I did when I came to law school was buy a brand-new laptop.

Each day, my Civ Pro professor would put four or five students in the hot seat and grill them mercilessly about the Federal Rules. The day before he had called on two people next to me, and I just knew I was next. So that night I prepared meticulously for class and assembled some pretty good notes on the reading.

The next day in class, the professor spent a good 40 minutes grilling another student. Glancing at the clock, I was pretty sure I was off the hook. But sure enough, just as I was about to heave a sigh of relief, I heard, "Why would the Federal Rules allow this? Mr. Khan?" No problem; I was ready. I had all my notes right in front of me. No problem, except for the fact that somewhere between "Mr." and "Khan" my laptop flashed a "warning: your battery is out of power; computer will now go to sleep" message. Ho-hum.

—JOSEPH J. KHAN, UNIVERSITY OF CHICAGO LAW SCHOOL

First, law professors use hypotheticals with great frequency, and you should try to write them down when possible to help you study for exams. (Professors often use similar hypotheticals on their exams.) Although the standard note-taking you learned in high school or college will serve you well as you attempt to write down a case's holding or a point raised by another student, hypotheticals are the backbone of a legal education in their ability to bring different factual scenarios to bear on a given legal principle.

Second, make sure that you write down case names and page references as you take notes on the discussion of a given topic in class. Many examinations are "open-book," and being able to locate a specific idea or quotation quickly may help you immensely when the test is given. In addition, this practice will help get you more comfortable with the idea of referring to cases as a matter of routine. While professors want to know what you think when you take a test, part of learning to think like a lawyer is the ability to find support in the law for your position. Thus, you do not simply want to say that "the Constitution gives courts the power of judicial review," but rather that "*Marbury v. Madison* announced that the Constitution gives courts the power of judicial review." Learning to refer to cases that stand for certain legal propositions is a skill you will find useful throughout your law school career.

ASKING QUESTIONS

Because casebook reading is often so difficult and the study of law initially so foreign, many students begin law school feeling that they are a little behind their peers. While undoubtedly there will be some pre-law majors in your class or people with prior legal experience, the great majority of students are similarly new to the study of law. It is important to remember this as you sit in class each day and attempt to digest the material. For there are few places where it is more accurate to say that if you do not understand what is going on, there are undoubtedly others similarly confused.

You may find in your classes that there are a handful of students who speak up regularly. Some of these students might be admired as thoughtful students who pore over the reading each night and come prepared to discuss it the following day. Others may be less well-liked if they "pounce" when a fellow student hesitates before answering or seem to be talking nearly as much as the professor. The line between being one who occasionally comments and what some students call a "gunner"—loosely speaking, one who talks not to have a question answered, but rather to indicate how smart he or she is—can be a fine one. While students should generally feel comfortable speaking up in class, if you find yourself talking many times each day, it may be wise to sit back and listen for a while.

Discretion is the better part of class participation. You must judiciously determine what sort of nickname you want, because you will have one. The most dreaded is "Helium Hand." Every class has at least two. The most prolific Helium Hand in my class earned the nickname early in first semester. The nickname, however, was not all that accurate because he chose not to raise his hand, but rather to speak out without being acknowledged by the professor. This went on for several weeks until one famous day in Torts.

Much like any other day, Torts was peppered with Helium Hand's usual quips. But on this day, the professor had reached his limit. After one outburst in the middle of class, he turned to Helium Hand and said, "Would you just shut up!" This brought the class to a complete stop because of the laughter and applause. Helium Hand was deflated for a few weeks, but, much like a phoenix, he rose again (although then he raised his hand instead of just blurting out his responses).

—DAVID E. CARNEY, WILLIAM & MARY SCHOOL OF LAW

The majority of law students do not talk a great deal in class; in fact, most students hardly speak at all. Classes thus become divided between the 15 or 20 students who may ask questions and the 100 or more who never do. It is useful to remind yourself from the very first day to speak up when you do not understand the material being discussed. Few things can be more daunting than raising your hand in front of your peers and admitting that you do not know what is going on. But it is often these questions—rather than the lengthy philosophical ones—that help the most students. If you are afraid of getting tongue-tied, hate speaking in public, or just cannot seem to formulate a question as well as some of the class's regular talkers, you should feel free to fall back on the standard "I'm sorry, I did not understand that. Can you repeat/clarify that for me?" You'll be surprised how many pens start to scribble when the professor answers you.

AVOIDING EMBARRASSMENT

In addition to doing and understanding your reading, preparing to be called on, and maximizing the value of your class experience, there are a few odds and ends that you should know before your first class begins. Some of these may seem obvious, others less so, but either way, remembering them can spare you embarrassment:

1. Juries return verdicts; judges render decisions.

2. Criminal suits involve the government charging an individual with a crime, and the crime is proven by guilt beyond a reasonable doubt. Civil suits tend to involve private parties suing each other (usually for money). The plaintiff wins not by showing guilt beyond a reasonable doubt, but rather by the lower standard of a preponderance of the evidence—it's more likely than not that the defendant did it.

3. A defendant in a civil suit is either liable or not liable. A defendant in a criminal suit is either guilty or not guilty.

4. Most judicial opinions open with the name of the judge who authored them: for instance, Scalia, J. The "J" is not the judge's first initial, but rather stands for Judge or Justice. "CJ" stands for Chief Judge or Chief Justice.

5. Many English cases have names such as *Regina v. Party X*. "Regina" is not a person's name but refers to the Queen.

—by Neal A. Potischman

CHAPTER 3

Preparing for Exams

CONQUERING THE FEAR

Law students, especially first-semester law students, often appear to be preoccupied with thoughts about examinations. Some of this preoccupation is well-founded: Law school exams are often comprehensive, challenging, and time-constrained. Moreover, unlike most college courses, your grade on just one exam often determines your grade for the entire course. On the other hand, many students' fears about law school exams are probably unnecessary. The exam-preparation and exam-taking skills that served you well in college undoubtedly provide a good base upon which to prepare for law school exams. To minimize your pre-exam anxieties, the following pages will provide insights into what you can expect law school exams to look like and suggestions for preparing yourself efficiently and effectively.

THE FORMAT AND STRUCTURE OF LAW SCHOOL EXAMS

THREE BASIC FORMATS

Law school professors administer exams in three basic formats: in-class exams, take-home exams, and extended take-home exams. In-class exams are administered during a limited time frame, such as 90 minutes or three hours. All students in the course complete the examination at the same time in the same room(s). Such exams offer the advantage of proceeding relatively quickly. However, many students find that the time constraints of in-class exams challenge their ability to formulate and organize their answers as completely as they would like. Such students might prefer the second type of exam, the take-home.

> *As final exams approach, I prefer to study somewhere else on campus. Most people are so nervous and are freaking out. "What page of your outline are you on?" "How long is your outline?" "Are you ready?" "I am so prepared." "It will be easy." "Oh, you are only on page 10 of your outline? That's okay. I am sure you will finish. You probably are more thorough than me." People like that make me nervous. By avoiding those people, I am able to focus on my work and not on everyone else.*
>
> —ADAM BERLIN, INDIANA UNIVERSITY-BLOOMINGTON
> SCHOOL OF LAW

Take-home examinations are often administered during one full day in which the student picks up the examination on campus during the morning, races home to work on the exam, and then returns the completed exam to campus late in the afternoon. Some students prefer this type of exam because they find it more relaxing to work in a private environment and believe that they have more of an opportunity to think about and organize their answers. Other students complain that take-home exams ask so many questions or such detailed questions that they induce just as much time pressure as in-class exams. At any rate, most professors give guidance or limits as to how many words students may use in answering each question. Staying within the word limit is sometimes the most challenging part of completing a take-home exam.

In the third type of exam, the extended take-home, students have an extended amount of time, such as a school's entire examination period (usually one to two weeks), to complete exam questions or write a paper on an assigned topic. Professors often expect the highest degree of organization and comprehensiveness on these exams. Many students prefer these exams because they allow students the greatest flexibility in deciding when to work on them. Other students are less fond of these types of exams because they penalize procrastination.

Knowing about the different types of exams scheduled for each course, some students pick their elective courses to emphasize one type of exam or another. It's best to let your own exam-taking strengths and weaknesses be your guide if and when you decide to make such choices. If you work well under time pressure, you might want to choose classes with in-class exams. Conversely, if you require more thinking and editing time, you might want to choose classes with take-home exams.

Fortunately (or unfortunately), as a One-L, you will have very little choice in which types of courses or exams you take. Your classes, except for maybe one elective, will likely be chosen for you (see Chapter 5, "Choosing Classes"), and your exams will be mostly in-class.

THREE TYPES OF QUESTIONS

As in college, you will complete exams with varied types of questions, including multiple-choice, short-answer, and essay questions. Although some students may question the value of multiple-choice questions, many professors use them precisely because students will face such questions on their bar exams. Short-answer questions allow professors to narrow focus and to hone in on knowledge of specific legal principles or public policy arguments. For example, a professor might ask you to explain briefly why you would support or oppose a proposed change to the Federal Rules of Civil Procedure. Longer essay questions allow professors to test students' ability to apply and combine a number of legal principles in the same answer. Accordingly, most exam questions require longer essay answers.

Essay questions often present a hypothetical set of facts from which students are expected to spot the contestable legal issues and to analyze each of them. Such questions are called "issue spotters." Success on issue spotters requires students to bear in mind the various legal topics discussed in a course while they read the hypothetical facts. Instead of asking students to comment on how the fact pattern relates to a particular course topic, the professor will require students to play the role of an attorney advising a client about his or her legal rights as they relate to the fact pattern or to play the role of a judge issuing an opinion about the legal disputes that would arise from the fact pattern. Therefore, the student must decide which topics (legal issues) must be addressed in answering the question.

USING NOTES AND STUDY AIDS

A final consideration worth noting about exam format and structure is that professors allow students to have varied levels of consultation with notes and other study aids while completing exams. Some exams, especially many in-class exams, are "closed-book," meaning they must be completed without any consultation with outlines, notes, casebooks, or other materials. However, most exams, especially take-home exams and extended take-home exams, are "open-book," meaning that students are allowed to consult outlines, class notes, casebooks, and other reference materials as they work. Even in open-book exams, students should bear in mind that time constraints may limit their ability to consult reference materials as much as they would like. Unless told otherwise, students should assume that they cannot consult or collaborate with other students or teachers concerning their exam answers.

Prepare from the Start

Given that so many law students are preoccupied with exam anxiety throughout the semester, it makes sense to start preparing for exam day from the first day of class. There are helpful steps you can take toward this end at every point in the semester—beginning, middle, or end. The following list of tips is offered as a guide. You should, of course, continue the practices that contributed to your success on college exams and consider how your own capacity for memorization, analysis, and recall may counsel against some of these suggestions. However, it's important to recognize that the amount of material you must study in order to prepare for law school exams will often far exceed the amount of material you had to study when preparing for college exams. This consideration alone makes it essential that you prepare for law school exams throughout the semester, rather than trying the legendary last-minute cram at the end of the semester.

Tips for the Beginning of the Semester

1. Create a Sensible Exam Schedule.

Although first-year students have few scheduling choices, at most law schools, second- and third-year students have considerable choice in choosing classes. When faced with such choices, you should undoubtedly choose courses and professors that seem interesting and relevant to your future career choices. However, you should also keep your examination schedule in mind when you choose your classes. For more information on this topic, see Chapter 5, "Choosing Classes."

Most law schools have mechanisms in place to ensure that students do not register for multiple classes that have exams scheduled for the same time. Beyond that, you may also want to think long and hard about choosing two courses that have in-class exams scheduled on the same day. Trying to keep straight the detailed rules of evidence in the morning when you have spent the previous evening studying for your afternoon tax exam may lead to suboptimal performance in both subjects. Scheduling your classes so that you have at least one night between each in-class exam should leave ample time to review for each subject, especially if you have worked to prepare yourself throughout the semester.

Many law students would also advise against scheduling one-day take-home exams on successive days. Although such scheduling would generally leave you with an evening during which to review for the second exam, the amount of energy spent in working on the first exam for an entire eight-hour (or perhaps 10-hour) period may deplete your energy for an exam the next day.

2. Review your professor's old exams and sample answers.

Although changes in the state of the law in a given area or in a professor's research interests can alter the substance of questions that a professor will ask from semester to semester, most professors ask the same type of questions repeatedly. Knowing early in the semester that your professor likes to ask policy questions (i.e., questions that ask you to evaluate the advantages and disadvantages of various legal doctrines) may lead you to focus less on the individual cases that you study during the semester and more on the commentary that is offered in each section of your casebook. Conversely, if you know your professor prefers issue spotters, you may want to concentrate throughout the semester on remembering general legal rules and case names so you will be prepared to resolve fine differences among cases. Finally, an early look at exams is valuable because it may enable you to determine whether your exam is likely to encompass all course topics or cover only a few areas in depth.

3. Assess the availability of study aids to help you master the course material.

From the day you arrive on campus for your first semester of law school, you will hear discussions about student outlines, commercial outlines, hornbooks, treatises, mini-treatises, case briefs, audio reviews, video reviews, and various other study aids. Students typically have one of two reactions to these materials. Some students immediately purchase as many of them as they can afford, thinking that the more materials they buy, the more information they will learn and the better they will perform on exams. Three months later, when they start their most serious exam preparation, many of these students will open their study aids for the very first time and determine that they simply don't have enough time to use the study aids effectively. Hence, these study aids will sit unused on the bookshelf or be resold to other students in a later semester.

> *Whatever commercial outline you purchase, be sure to use it diligently. Also, don't freak out and buy each one on the market. Although you might strengthen the economy, it will only take too much of your valuable and scarce time to read each one. Find one that follows your casebook or purchase a general one applicable to the entire subject.*
>
> —ADAM BERLIN, INDIANA UNIVERSITY-BLOOMINGTON
> SCHOOL OF LAW

Other students resist the temptation to buy any study aids. These students might think that the aids are not "academic" and that using them will somehow compromise the student's academic integrity. Alternatively, students might not want to spend any more money than they have already spent on their textbooks, or they might think that they can and will learn everything they need to know by reading their casebooks and attending class.

Neither set of students has necessarily taken the most helpful course of action. Most students will find it useful (if not indispensable) to consult study aids for some of their courses. Sometimes professors will even recommend aids or, in rare instances, may assign reading from them to supplement casebook reading. However, study aids are not meant as a substitute for assigned readings and do not purport to convey the same information. They often lack information on recent cases or statutory changes. Moreover, they convey the authors' assessment of the meaning of various cases and statutes, and the authors' assessment may be quite different from that of your casebook author or your professor. With this in mind, what are the various types of study aids, and what are the benefits of each one?

STUDENT OUTLINES

> *I didn't learn about the value of student outlines until my second year—one year too late, I think. If you can find a relatively recent (less than three years old), detailed student outline from the same course and same professor, you've hit gold. I bring my student outline to class and take notes on it, comparing what the professor is saying now to what he or she said then. It is immensely helpful when preparing for a cold call and equally helpful when preparing your own outline or studying for an exam. I probably wasted an extra hour preparing each night my first year because I didn't have any student outlines. I wish somebody had told me how valuable they were.*
>
> —GREG GOTTESMAN, HARVARD LAW SCHOOL

Student outlines, created by individual students or groups of students who have taken one of your courses during a previous semester, generally provide organized notes about the course's readings and class discussions. They may also incorporate notes from other study aids that the student outliner consulted during the course. While they can never convey all the information offered in the reading, they may help you pinpoint the most important parts of major cases or discover before going to class the professor's particular interpretation of the importance of a case. The primary advantage of student outlines over other study aids is that they are geared toward your particular course and will therefore likely cover the same cases that you are reading and similar comments that your professor will make during class. They may also be quite inexpensive compared to commercial study aids. Student outlines may be available for purchase at your law school copy center or bookstore or may be available from student organizations or from friends who are in their second or third year of law school.

COMMERCIAL OUTLINES

Commercial outlines, often created by groups of lawyers or legal researchers, provide organized discussions of major cases and ideas in various areas of law. Some of the major commercial outlines are indexed to tell you which parts of the outline correspond to which pages of the casebook you might be using in your course. As such, the outlines purport to help you summarize and understand the most important rules conveyed in the most important cases in a given subject area. They also help you understand arguments that a court might have considered and rejected in deciding a particular case. The primary advantage of commercial outlines over other study aids is that they try to present a fair amount of detail about major cases, often including a discussion of dissenting opinions. They also try to organize cases in a way that will help you understand how legal doctrines have evolved in a particular area.

Emanuel and *Gilbert* publish the most popular commercial outlines. You can consult with older students to find out which one is best for a particular subject (also see "Andy's Picks," below, for one expert's view on the best commercial materials). For example, many students recommend *Emanuel's* outline for Constitutional Law, but recommend *Gilbert's* outline for Property. Glance through an outline before purchasing it to make sure it has what you need and that it is organized in a way that makes sense to you.

HORNBOOKS, TREATISES, AND MINI-TREATISES

Hornbooks, treatises, and mini-treatises, often created by law professors, are much like undergraduate textbooks. Organized in chapters by issue, these sources seek to provide a historical discussion about how the law has evolved in a given area and to tell you the significant rules that are stated in major cases, without providing you with many of the factual details. In addition, these sources serve as good reference tools for conducting further research on legal issues. The sources tend to have many lengthy footnotes that can alert you to related cases, books, and law review articles. Their primary advantage over other study aids is that they are written in understandable prose (most of the time) and highlight important trends and scholarly insights into the area of law that you are studying. Therefore, they often serve as one of the most efficient sources from which to gain a basic understanding of the evolution of legal doctrines in a particular area. In addition, especially because of their detailed footnotes, they tend to be much more comprehensive than student outlines or commercial outlines. However, their comprehensiveness can limit their usefulness. On any given topic, they are likely to reference many cases and other reference tools that neither your casebook nor your professor will reference. Moreover, a chapter on a given topic in a treatise or hornbook often includes a lot more reading than the total amount of required class reading on the topic. On balance, your professors are more likely to recommend hornbooks and treatises than other commercial study aids because they are considered to present a more comprehensive discussion than alternative aids. There are several excellent treatises, most notably Laurence Tribe's treatise on Constitutional Law.

AUDIO AND VIDEO REVIEWS

Most law school bookstores sell audiotapes and videotapes that serve as study aids for law school courses, especially the basic first-year courses. These tapes often consist of lectures given by leading professors in the particular course you have chosen. The tapes are interesting in that they enable you to hear leading experts describe the important issues in their field in their own words. The tapes also enable you to process information without the same type of effort that you might expend in reading. For example, students sometimes listen to the audiotapes while they work out at the gym or while they are on a long airplane or automobile ride. On the other hand, these sources might be the most limited in terms of the amount of information that they can convey. Moreover, they tend to impose limitations on your ability to quickly choose the particular section that you want to hear or view at one time. Instead, for continuity purposes, many students indicate that audiotapes and videotapes are best suited for review of an entire course at the end of the semester when a student is able to derive benefit from all of the contents of the tapes at one time. For example, Arthur Miller's Civil Procedure tapes serve as an excellent end-of-course review for learning one of the more difficult first-year classes. A final consideration in the possible purchase of these sources is that they are often quite expensive and are not as likely to be consulted in your future career as would a treatise.

OTHER STUDY AIDS

A number of other study aids might be available at your particular law school. For instance, some law schools offer workshops to first-year students on exam-taking skills or on the substance of particular first-year courses. Some of the organizations that offer bar review courses to recent law school graduates also offer workshops to first-year students on both exam-taking skills and the substance of first-year courses. In addition, some law schools offer students access to computer programs that have sample exam questions and answers.

In short, there are a lot of study aids from which to choose. The best advice is to plan early in the semester which study aids you will use for a particular course and then to employ them at the time that makes the most sense. Opening a treatise three days before an exam is probably useless because it has too much information to wade through in a short amount of time. However, using a treatise to supplement your reading and class notes at the end of each course topic might really help you sort through all the cases and rules. Listening to eight hours of audiotapes about the Federal Rules of Civil Procedure might be useless when you have only studied one or two of the rules. However, by the end of the semester, when you have learned dozens of rules, an audiotape might provide a low-stress refresher on how the various rules fit together.

Andy Metheny, who has managed Harvard Law School's Coop for the past six years, has become an "expert" on commercial study aids. He has sold thousands of study aids and listened to students brag about the best ones and return the worst. Many students at Harvard Law School use him as a resource during the first year. His overall selections for the best first-year study aids are listed below. His top pick is listed first, followed by his second pick, and so on.

Andy's Picks

Civil Procedure: *Civil Procedure: Examples and Explanations* by Joseph Glannon; *Emanuel*; *E-Z Rules for Civil Procedure*; *Sum and Substance* Civil Procedure audiotapes by Arthur Miller (but Andy warns that audiotapes in general are more expensive than most other study aids)

Constitutional Law: *Emanuel*; Laurence Tribe's Constitutional Law treatise

Contracts: *Contracts* by Marvin Chirelstein; E. Allan Farnsworth's Contracts treatise; *Emanuel* or *Gilbert*

Criminal Law: *Understanding Criminal Law* by Joshua Dressler; *Emanuel* or *Gilbert*

Criminal Procedure: *Understanding Criminal Procedure* by Joshua Dressler; *Emanuel* or *Gilbert*

Property: *Gilbert*

Torts: *Prosser and Keeton on Torts* (hornbook); *The Law of Torts: Examples and Explanations* by Joseph Glannon; *Emanuel* or *Gilbert*

General: Also consider Legalines or Casenotes for daily preparation; BarCharts for quick overall review of courses (especially for One-L courses)

TIPS TO FOLLOW THROUGHOUT THE SEMESTER

1. READ YOUR ASSIGNMENTS REGULARLY.

Make no mistake, law classes require a lot of reading. Sometimes first-semester students are deceived when they see reading assignments of 20 to 30 pages per class. They might be tempted to believe that if they fall a little behind, they will be able to catch up at a later date. The reason that they have been deceived is that they may not realize that it takes a lot longer to read and understand 20 pages of case law than 20 pages of a history textbook or a novel. Unlike a textbook or a novel, which is probably organized to culminate in the assertion of a specific point, a legal case is organized to convey a lot of information that may be tangential to what you ultimately need to understand after reading the case. Cases may discuss facts, jurisdictional issues, and arguments that the court has rejected. Often this information masks the more important "rule" conveyed by the case and requires students to spend extra time seeking out the rule. Every case is assigned for a reason. It is important to allow yourself enough time to read the case and to reflect upon why it is important. In addition, in many law school classes, the professor may call on you to discuss the case at any unexpected time. Most professors (and classmates) will be sympathetic if they can tell that you have read a case, even if you do not understand its nuances. However, their sympathies will likely diminish significantly if it appears that you have not attempted to prepare for class.

2. TAKE NOTES ABOUT THE CASES THAT YOU READ.

As mentioned in Chapter 2, "Preparing for Class," one excellent way to study for exams during the semester is to brief your cases.

Some first-semester students type or write formal half-page (or longer) briefs of every case that they read. Other students write less formal notes about each case in the margins of their casebooks. Because you will bring your casebook to class, it is easy to refer to notes that you have made in the margins when you are discussing a particular case. Some students prefer this method of taking notes because it is less time-consuming than writing a more formal case brief. Additionally, it encourages students to refer to the actual language of the case when they look back at their notes about the case.

Neither of these methods—briefing or taking less formal notes in your casebook—is necessarily superior. You might want to try both during the first semester. The important thing is to develop some method for recording notes about the cases that you read. This will assist you in participating in and following class discussions. It will also assist you in refining any notes or outlines that you decide to create and use in preparing for final exams.

3. TAKE COPIOUS CLASS NOTES.

It is important to understand and record what you hear in class. Your professor's perspective on the importance of a case, and his or her approval or disapproval of the way it was decided, can be crucial in understanding cases and in thinking about the types of issues that you are likely to encounter on your final exam. Moreover, many professors are skilled in facilitating classroom discussion to reflect a variety of viewpoints on the issues that you study in each case. Therefore, the comments that fellow students make about the reasoning in each case, and the implications of the decision, can help you think about and understand perspectives that you might not have otherwise considered. There are multiple sides to every issue. The adversary nature of our legal system is built upon this fundamental belief. Use class discussion and create class notes that will help you understand and recall the multiple sides of each issue.

4. Review your readings and notes frequently.

One of the pitfalls of the fact that many law school classes require exams only at the end of the semester is that students are tempted to move from week to week and topic to topic without reviewing what they have learned. They already feel like they spend a great deal of time reading and preparing for class each day. Therefore, they do not spend any time on the "extra work" entailed in reviewing what they have already completed. This is a mistake. Precisely because law school exams test a full semester's worth of work, it is imperative to review each section of the course as you complete it. Although the topics in various sections of law school courses often build on each other, students can often identify the most important issues in each section of the course after they complete it. Paying specific attention to legal questions that appear to be unresolved by the cases you have read will help you focus your attention in later sections of the course and may be an indication of potential exam questions.

5. Consult with other people.

It is difficult, if not impossible, for any one student to master all the doctrine and policy issues in a course merely by reading and attending class. Inevitably, you will misinterpret a key case or forget how a prior decision influenced a court's reasoning. No matter how hard you try, you can never get everything that the professor says into your notes correctly. For these reasons, and because your entire legal career will be filled with consultations with other people, you should take the opportunity to confer with your professors and, more importantly, with other students throughout the semester.

COMMUNICATING WITH YOUR PROFESSORS

In college, you might have avoided talking with professors because your peers would have called you a "brown-noser." Unfortunately, some of the same peer pressure exists in law school. And that's not the only stumbling block to dealing with law school professors. Another reason many students do not communicate with their professors is the intimidation associated with the Socratic Method. But you really should not allow these feelings to stand in the way of getting to know your professors, especially if you feel that such contact is important to your learning some of the more difficult points of law. Most law professors will be more than willing to talk with you. In many ways, you share more in common with your law professors than you might have with your college professors. They all completed law school at some time, and now they are helping you to become part of their profession.

There are a variety of ways to ask questions of your professors. Professors generally respond to questions during class. Many professors will also entertain questions for a short period after a class ends. In addition, most law schools require professors to hold office hours during which students can stop by on an individual basis. Finally, many law schools are working diligently to acquaint their students with the conveniences of modern technology that may be useful to them in their legal practice. Therefore, professors often accept and respond to questions over e-mail and may create bulletin boards on the Internet upon which all students can post questions that the professor and other students can read and answer.

COMMUNICATING WITH OTHER STUDENTS: STUDY GROUPS

> *My first year in law school, I studied for Constitutional Law and Criminal Law with four other people. We used to meet at Starbuck's on 67th Street and Columbus Avenue in New York City. Most groups studied in the library, but not us; we liked to be in public when we studied. One of our favorite ways to review was to use Gilbert's flash cards. The flash cards asked questions by setting up ridiculous scenarios using literary and other popular characters. Invariably, wherever we sat down, tables seemed to empty around us. Coffee-drinking New Yorkers are smart enough to know that they should avoid law school students armed with Gilbert's flash cards.*
>
> —GABRIELLE KLEINMAN, COLUMBIA LAW SCHOOL

Within the first week or two of the first semester of law school, you are bound to hear students forming "study groups." Some students put a lot of thought into choosing a group to work with, hoping to gain an advantage in understanding class materials. The size of these groups varies, from two to as many as 10 participants (more than 10 people is probably inefficient). Some study groups meet daily, others weekly or monthly. The length of the meetings also varies, from 30 minutes to two hours or more. A study group may merely discuss class readings or may decide to create group notes or a group outline of the course.

Being in a study group is usually a good idea. Discussing course topics with other students on a regular basis is bound to increase your understanding of class materials. In forming a study group, however, know exactly what it is that you want to accomplish and choose other students who have the same goals. Most importantly, team up with people who you think you will enjoy working with and who will enjoy working with you. Do not give in to the temptation to choose the person in the class who strikes you as the most brilliant, unless you truly think that you will enjoy spending time with that person. Your assessment of that person's brilliance may be inaccurate and, if you really do not appreciate the person's company, you are likely to be too annoyed and distracted to glean much benefit from studying with that individual.

Here are three suggestions for working in a study group:

1. USE YOUR TIME EFFICIENTLY.

This goal can be achieved by agreeing to parameters up front. If you agree to spend an hour together for each class each week, you are likely to accomplish more during an hour than you would if you had not decided the duration of your meeting in advance.

2. PREPARE FOR YOUR MEETINGS IN ADVANCE.

Each study group member should review his or her notes and other class materials before the meeting. Determining in advance what issues seem most important or most confusing will provide focus for study group meetings.

3. ESTABLISH AND STICK TO A MEETING SCHEDULE.

Whether you decide to meet monthly, weekly, or more than once a week, stick to your schedule. Think of law school as your job and your study group meetings as important appointments. Missing several meetings may mean more work come finals.

TIPS FOR THE FINAL WEEKS OF THE SEMESTER

1. ORGANIZE YOUR VARIOUS NOTES AND STUDY AIDS.

One common panic expressed by law students at the end of the semester is that they have accumulated so much information for each course that they do not know where to start. You should bear this in mind as you approach the end of the semester in each of your classes. Organize all class notes, reading notes, handouts, and pertinent information from any extra study aids by topic or by date. Having all relevant materials together will enable you to easily cross-reference your various sources as you review individual topics in a course.

Going one step further, you might want to consider outlining the information you have accumulated for each course. You might choose to outline the whole course yourself, or to split the course into sections with members of your study group or with other class members. The advantage of doing the outline yourself is that you will review all sections of the course while you create the outline, and you will be able to include what you perceive to be the most important information in your own words. On the other hand, group outlines will require less of your time, which you can then spend reviewing other important materials.

2. Make your outline readable, not a masterpiece.

Many students perceive the outline as a work of art in and of itself and strive to create something that is both thorough enough and "pretty" enough that they would be comfortable turning it in for a grade. Being such a perfectionist is both stressful and unnecessary. An outline should serve as a reference tool that enables you to remember what you read and what you heard in class without referring back to the casebook or to your notes. In many cases, the shorter the outline, the better. Being able to condense a week's worth of course materials into one page of an outline probably shows that you can remember how the week's materials fit together, which is far more important than the tiny details of each day and each case. Moreover, the shorter you make the outline, the easier it will be to find points that you want to look for on a test.

3. Work through old exams with classmates.

As mentioned earlier in this chapter, working through old exams is one of the best ways to review for your exams, especially in the final days. Not only does working through the exams give you a sense of the types of questions that your professor is likely to ask and of the time constraints involved in answering the questions, it also can guide you in thinking about and reviewing many of the topics you discussed in your course.

Review the exams with other classmates, especially if the professor does not provide sample answers. Other students will spot and consider points that you might have missed. After discussing these points with your fellow classmates, you probably won't miss these key issues when it counts.

Also, when completing old exams, practice under timed conditions. You don't want to be surprised on the day of the exam when the proctor calls time. By practicing with time constraints, you will figure out just how much time you can spend spotting issues, outlining, and writing on the various parts of your professor's old exams.

4. TRY TO GET THE ENTIRE COURSE DOWN INTO ONE PAGE.

On the day before the exam, some students find it helpful to boil the entire course down into one page. For example, Contracts may be condensed into a series of questions with some bullet points. The major questions might include: Was there a contract? Was there a breach? What are the potential remedies? The point of this exercise is to rise above the trees, so that you can see the forest. Professors will be more lenient if they think you get the "big picture" on an exam, even if you miss some key issues; they will not be so conciliatory if you spend the majority of your test time in the weeds, citing facts from irrelevant cases.

5. SET REALISTIC GOALS.

As you plan how to spend those last few weeks or last few days of the semester, set realistic goals. Although it is important to put a lot of preparation into your exams, it is also important to be realistic about what you can accomplish in your final push. If you have followed some of the suggestions above, you probably have prepared yourself well for your exams throughout the semester. Treat the last few days leading up to your exams as an opportunity to review what you have already studied, rather than a furious push to learn a lot of information that you did not master during the semester. To that end, do not try to do too much. Your exams, because of the time constraints involved with in-class exams and because of the extended period of time during which you must concentrate on take-home exams, are almost as much an endurance test as they are a test of legal knowledge. Remember to sleep and to eat healthfully during the days leading up to exams so that you will be as alert as possible. Trying to cram in an extra few hours of studying at the expense of a decent night's sleep might seem like a good idea while you are doing it, but not such a great idea when you are thinking about how badly you want to nap during your Civil Procedure take-home.

—by Jim Trilling

CHAPTER 4

Tips for Taking Exams

> *During my first year in law school, there was a general feeling among the male students that my Civil Procedure professor preferred women to men. In the hope that my professor would think he was grading a woman's exam, and would therefore give the student a better grade, an industrious male friend of mine tried to make the professor think he was grading a female's exam. When time was called at the end of the exam, my male friend literally plucked the longest hairs he could find right out of his head and placed them gently in the middle of his exam book. He boasted about this to me after the exam, convinced that he would get a higher grade if the professor found those hairs. I guess some people will try anything to circumvent the anonymous grading system used on law school exams!*
>
> —MICHELE SIANO, BROOKLYN LAW SCHOOL

SURVIVING FIRST-YEAR EXAMS

Whether you take time off before going to law school or go directly to law school after college, law school exams are unnerving. An *entire* semester of material—weeks and weeks of cases, statutes, theories, and policies—crammed into one test upon which your *entire* grade rests. If being called on blindly in class makes you uncomfortable because of the pressure, wait until you experience your first round of exams! Surviving exams is probably the most difficult aspect of the first year in law school. Below are some tips to help you survive and prosper.

KNOWING IT COLD IS NOT ENOUGH

Without a doubt, the most important tip regarding test-taking is to know the material as well as humanly possible. That goes without saying. Even when you know the material, you still face the challenge of being able to perform well on an exam—that is, to prove to the professor that you know everything you do. A common complaint among law school students is that their exam grades do not reflect how well they knew the material. "I cannot believe I didn't do better on that exam. I knew that material *cold*."

The reality is that knowing the material cold is not enough. Doing well on a law school exam also requires strategizing and taking certain critical precautionary measures. A quick walk-through of the types of things you should do immediately before, during, and after the exam should help you do as well on an exam as you think you should or, perhaps, do better than you thought possible.

THREE PRE-EXAM TIPS

1. STAY COMFORTABLE AND FOCUSED.

The day of an exam is usually a stressful one. The key to doing well on the exam, therefore, is remaining as comfortable and focused as you can. A number of things can help you achieve that comfort level on the big day. First of all, make sure that you get to school early. If you are prone to oversleeping, set two alarm clocks for yourself or make a deal with a fellow classmate that you will call each other in the morning. The point is that you don't want to feel rushed or panicked about being late. Getting to school about a half-hour before the exam starts will allow you to clear your head and relax before the exam begins. If you get there just as time is called, your mind probably will not be focused enough. Unless you have unusually good bladder control, avoid drinking too many liquids the day of the exam, particularly caffeine-laden ones. One of the biggest pressures you face on a law school exam is the pressure of time. Five or 10 minutes wasted on trips to the bathroom is unnecessary and can even be fatal in a short one- or two-hour exam.

2. DON'T STUDY ON THE DAY OF THE EXAM.

Some students think the best way to prepare for an exam is to study every possible moment—right up to when the exam begins. Big mistake. Unless the exam is in the late afternoon, you should organize your study schedule around the presumption that you will *not* study for the exam at all during the day of the exam. The closer you get to the exam, the more nervous you probably will become and the less likely you are to remember what you study. Go to bed the night before an exam feeling confident that you have learned all that you can and that you know the material as well as possible.

Likewise, discussing the material with your friends right before an exam is a bad idea. Hashing out disagreements and different interpretations of the material with your classmates is useful during the semester. Two minutes before an exam it will only confuse and distract you.

3. BRING A SNACK AND EARPLUGS.

> *I was so nervous before my Contracts exam that I could not eat even though the final was not until 1 P.M. As I was getting through the first question, I noticed that I was getting hungry; by the second question, my stomach was rumbling; by the third question, I was STARVING! My stomach was*

> *howling for food! The moral of the story is eat before*
> *the exam or take something in with you!*
>
> —Amy Thompson, Indiana University-Bloomington
> School of Law

Before you head off to take the exam, make sure that you have a few key items. To ensure that you have everything you need, you can even make yourself a checklist. First and foremost, if your school uses a numbering system for exams or requires identification cards, remember to bring your exam identification number and/or identification card. Second, if you have not eaten, bring a snack. The snack should not be a full meal, but just enough to keep you energized. A granola bar, bagel, or even a candy bar is perfect. The other items on your checklist could include: extra pens and pencils; watch/clock that has a second hand; bottled water; and tissues (in case you or a neighbor has the sniffles).

Some students highly recommend earplugs, which can greatly improve your ability to concentrate during a law school exam. Even though you thought ahead to bring water and tissues, many of your ill-prepared classmates probably will not. As noted several times, a critical factor to success on a law school exam is concentration. It is impossible to concentrate and think clearly when you are distracted by the noise of dozens of other stressed-out law school students.

> *I will never forget my first law school exam. There*
> *were 125 of us packed into a room. I took a deep*
> *breath and tried to relax as I began. No more than*
> *five minutes into the exam, however, the woman*
> *to my right began sniffling—something she*
> *continued to do for the full three hours of the exam.*
> *Shortly thereafter, the man to my left started*

coughing. An unidentified person in front of me began writing with what I imagine was a lead pencil but sounded like a cat scratching wildly on a post. Needless to say, my concentration faltered. After that horrible experience, I never took an exam without wearing earplugs.

—Jodi Golinsky, Brooklyn Law School

My first year, second semester, I came down with a terrible cold a few days before my Constitutional Law exam. I was terrified, because often when I get sick, the cold clogs my brain as well as my sinuses, and I stare slack-jawed at people and the written word—hardly an ideal state in which to take an exam. As it turned out, however, my brain did me the favor of staying clear. The same could not be said of my nose and throat. I coughed, hacked, sneezed, gulped juice, and sniffed throughout the four hours of the exam. In between minor explosions and frenzied scrambles for tissues, not to mention labored breathing, I noticed the hapless souls around me looking equally miserable—not because they were also sick, but because I was making such an incredible racket. I felt very sorry for them, but there wasn't a lot I could do about it. I ended up doing fine. Of course, I had earplugs, and therefore the noise, at least, wasn't disrupting my concentration. My neighbors probably ended up worse off than I did; not only did they have to listen to me, but they also probably caught the cold.

—Elizabeth MacDonald, Stanford Law School

Ten Tips For Exam Day

1. Manage your time wisely.

Because law school exams are timed, a law school student's first instinct upon receiving the exam is to get started. While it is important to get going as soon as possible, there are two simple things you should do *before* getting started that will only take a few minutes—time worth spending. As soon as you get the exam, check to make sure you have the entire exam and that no pages or questions are missing. Although not a common occurrence, it is certainly possible that the person who stapled the exams together may have missed a page or two. Once you are sure you have the whole exam, see how many questions there are and apportion your time accordingly. Usually, the professor will indicate how much time you should spend on each question. Make a notation on each question when your time is up for that question. Pace yourself accordingly, *even if it means leaving some questions before you feel you have finished them entirely.* The worst thing you can do is spend so much time on certain questions that you do not have enough time to finish the entire exam. Writing down the time at which you must move on keeps you focused up front and conscious of your time constraints. Remember that the professor will only allot a certain number of points for each question. Getting full credit for one question and no credit for the others is not as good as two-thirds credit for each!

If possible, try to allot some time (about 10 to 15 minutes) for a quick reread at the end of an exam. Final rereads will allow you to make the necessary grammatical improvements. Moreover, flashes of brilliance on one question often come after you have finished working on the others.

> *Second year, first semester, I finished my Civil Procedure II exam right on time (I thought) and waited for the registrar to come and pick it up. No*

> *one came. I looked at the clock; it was five minutes
> past what I thought marked the end of the exam,
> and still no registrar. The other students were still
> working, which should have told me something,
> but I was rather slow that day. I began to idly leaf
> through the exam, twiddling my thumbs. As I heard
> the registrar's steps begin to come up the stairs,
> I realized I had missed the call of the question. I
> also realized that the exam had not been over, and
> instead of staring stupidly at the other students,
> I should have been answering the damn question
> right in the 10 minutes I had. Standing over my
> paper, I scrawled something illegible—to this day
> I don't know how the professor read it. And now
> I check the time that the exam ends very carefully.
> Being squeezed at the end of an exam is nothing
> new, but it shouldn't be because you can't tell time.*
>
> —Elizabeth MacDonald, Stanford Law School

2. Use IRAC.

A "good" answer on a law school exam inevitably contains a clear articulation of the issue and the rules or laws that apply to that issue, a detailed analysis and application of the facts at hand to the issue and rule, and, finally, a conclusion. This type of answer—one that contains the issue, rule, application/analysis, and conclusion— is called the "IRAC" method. Most professors subscribe to IRAC, and it is a useful way of thinking about what is important to cover in an answer. In a typical fact pattern on an exam, you will spot many, many issues—you would use the IRAC method to discuss each of these issues, usually in the order in which they appear.

The "issue" piece of IRAC is important because it demonstrates your ability to read a fact pattern and see what legal implications arise from the fact pattern. Being able to spot the correct issues in a complex set of facts is half the battle on a law school exam. Once you know the legal issue, the rules/laws that apply to that issue should be clear to you (after all that studying and memorizing). Applying and analyzing the law you know to the facts and issues in the exam is the most rigorous part of the examination process because it is something for which you do not have the answer ahead of time. Although the cases and materials discussed and studied in class will be relevant, it is highly unlikely that you will be working with a scenario on an exam that is an exact replica of anything you have thus far examined. You simply must go through your *own* analysis of the facts and circumstances and arrive at a logical and reasonable conclusion. Many students obsess about getting the answer "right" on a law school exam. Focusing on the correctness of an answer misses the point. Indeed, in most cases there is no single correct answer. Your grade will depend on how many issues you spotted and how well you analyzed those issues, not so much on the conclusions reached.

Following is a quick summary of IRAC and an example (using IRAC) based on the issue covered in the sample brief in Chapter 2, "Preparing for Class."

IRAC IN A NUTSHELL

IRAC has four major components, which are listed in question form below.

Issue: What is the legal issue?

Rule: What is the general rule (and any important sub-rules or exceptions) relating to that issue?

Application/Analysis: How do the specific facts in the fact pattern relate to the legal rule just mentioned? What are the key counterarguments and facts that would support such counterarguments?

Conclusion: What do you think the most likely legal result will be? What do you think the legal result should be?

Example of IRAC: The first issue is whether Jane has a right to keep the wolf that she captured in the hinterlands or whether the wolf belongs to the farmer who wounded and was chasing the wolf. The general rule is that wild animals are possessed only when they are captured, although the mortal wounding of an animal does give possession to the pursuer. See *Pierson v. Post.* In this case, there is a question about whether the wolf was "wild." Although Jane found the wolf on uninhabited land (where many "wild" wolves are known to roam), the facts suggest that the farmer's son considered this wolf a "pet." There is also a question about whether the wolf was killed by Jane or "mortally wounded" by the farmer. Although Jane struck the final blow to the wolf's midsection, the wolf would likely have died anyway because of the farmer's gunshot to the wolf's leg. In this case, I think possession of the wolf should be given to the farmer, because the farmer's son considered the wolf a "pet" and because the gunshot wound was probably fatal.

3. READ THE QUESTION CAREFULLY AND ANSWER WHAT IS ASKED.

Once you have IRAC down, it is critical to remember that a "good" answer is also one that responds to the question asked. Many law school students make the mistake of writing down everything they know about a particular topic irrespective of the question being asked on the topic. Don't make that mistake. Professors will not be impressed that you know all the material covered in the course. Professors want intelligent, thorough answers to the questions they have asked. Read the question very carefully and make sure you answer it directly.

4. READ THE FACT PATTERN TWICE BEFORE ANSWERING THE QUESTION.

Before you can answer the question most efficiently and effectively, you need to get a general feel for what the fact pattern is about, who the major players are, and so on. To do that, you should first quickly read through the fact pattern without writing anything down. Then go back and reread the fact pattern more carefully. On the second read, mark up the fact pattern and identify all the key issues (in the margins, preferably with different color ink). This second read, when you are determining what the key issues are and how the facts relate to those issues, will most likely determine your grade on the final.

5. JOT DOWN A QUICK OUTLINE BEFORE YOU BEGIN WRITING.

Knowing where your answer is going *before* you begin to write is important because you do not want to be three-quarters of the way through and realize that you need to change your conclusion or perhaps add an issue that you forgot as you were busy demonstrating your facility with the Rule Against Perpetuities. As precious as time is during an exam, the time taken to outline an answer is not wasted. In fact, it may save you time by helping you organize your thoughts.

One side note: The outline should *not* be detailed. It should contain just enough information about the key issues and other insights to guide you in writing your essay. Don't waste time writing an itemized outline that your professor will never see or grade.

6. LOOK FOR THE KEY ISSUES COVERED DURING THE COURSE.

Your professor will most likely test you on many, if not all, of the key areas covered in your course. If you have a syllabus or have completed a one-page outline of the key issues, you can check them off as you go through your exam. If your exam is missing one of the highlights of the course, you should glance through the fact patterns again—you may have missed something. Moreover, your professor probably will not have you discuss the same legal issue in two separate fact patterns, so watch out if you are spending most of your time discussing the same issue twice.

7. ON POLICY QUESTIONS, USE "BUZZ" WORDS AND CATCH PHRASES.

If you were a non-science major in college, you should light up when you see a policy question. The same rules apply here as in your undergraduate exams. If your professor loves certain words or ideas, this is the place to use them and even to underline them. Even on non-policy questions, your professor's scoring sheet may actually contain certain "buzz" words or key phrases. Don't keep the professor guessing. If a "buzz" word is warranted, write it down!

8. WRITE ON ONE SIDE OF THE PAGE AND SKIP EVERY OTHER LINE.

You are bound to forget something as you work through your test. By leaving lots of room, you have space to go back and add important issues or insights. If you do add something to an earlier section of your test, don't worry—the professor is not going to grade you down for a lack of symmetry on the page. By the way, if you choose to follow this method, ask for extra bluebooks before the exam starts. You don't want to be scrambling to the front of the room for extra bluebooks with only minutes left.

9. REMEMBER YOUR AUDIENCE.

The professor who will eventually read and grade your exam should be no stranger to you. You have spent an entire semester looking at this subject matter from her or his vantage point. Get into that professor's head. If there are certain doctrines and/or policies that your professor has stressed in class, make sure you incorporate them into your answer. Professors are humans too, after all. At bottom, they are sometimes humans with a penchant for appreciating those who agree with their point of view. Knowing the law and how to apply it means you will do well. Applying it in precisely the same manner as your professor would means you will do even better. If you want to disagree with your professor on an exam, make sure that you have adequately shown that you fully understand the professor's viewpoint before delving into your take on a key issue.

10. WRITE DOWN SOMETHING.

Many students will run out of time before finishing one of their first-year exams. The key is not to panic. Monitor your time carefully. If you do not have enough time to finish one of the questions, do *not* leave it blank. Your goal in these situations is partial credit. Write down your outline. Write down the key issues. Write down something!

Most professors understand the time crunch and will take pity if they see that you understood the key issues in the question. But they can't take pity on you if there's nothing staring at them on the page.

AFTER THE EXAM

> *After my Torts exam, my section went to a nearby pub to celebrate. Over a beer, a sectionmate and I started discussing the exam. He began to go into detail about the battery issue in the first question. Battery issue? I had missed it completely. I started freaking out. I was sure I had flunked. He said, "I hate to say it, Shan, but it's not a good thing that you missed that issue."*
>
> *Three weeks and much self-beratement later, I got my exam back. I tentatively peered at my score— full points on the first question. I guess battery wasn't an issue after all. The experience taught me not to discuss exams when they are over, but just to move on to greener pastures, or the next exam. . . .*
>
> —SHANNON GOTTESMAN, BOSTON COLLEGE LAW SCHOOL

Believe it or not, even though the exam is over, there is one additional "test-taking tip" that is critical. After the exam, leave immediately. Do *not* stop to talk with friends and colleagues about the exam. There is nothing worse than finishing an exam and then freaking out because your best friend Sally discussed something in her answer that you did not even see in the fact pattern. And it happens every time when you meet and chit-chat about the exam. Make a pact with your friends early on that no matter how tempted you are, you will not discuss the exam once it is over. Move on. You have more important things to worry about—things that you can actually control.

—by Jodi Golinsky

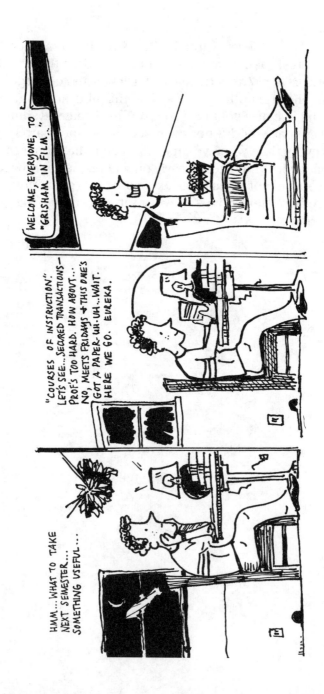

CHAPTER 5

Choosing Classes

> *My best class at law school was Tax. Yes, Tax! The reason was simple: My professor was great. Professor Warren could make any subject come alive, but you could tell he especially loved Tax. When the person in the front of the room is having such a good time, it's hard not to want to join in the fun. The class met earlier than any other at Harvard Law School, but I don't think I ever missed a session. No one did.*
>
> —GREG GOTTESMAN, HARVARD LAW SCHOOL

FIRST-YEAR CURRICULUM

Thanks to the renowned creativity of the legal profession, you'll be taking the same first-year courses as Atticus Finch and Bill Clinton. And you won't have a choice, except for maybe one elective.

Your first-year schedule will consist of the following courses, with little exception:

- Civil Procedure
- Contracts

- Criminal Law/Criminal Procedure
- Property
- Torts

Some schools will also require Constitutional Law and a legal research and writing course. But that's usually it.

If your school does allow you to choose an elective, here are a few tips. (Please use these tips in conjunction with the more general tips in the following section on choosing second- and third-year courses.) First, if you have not already taken a legal research and writing course, now may be a good time, especially if you're planning to work in law over your first summer. Legal writing is different from normal-person writing. That's why a lot of laypeople hate lawyers. Legal research is also difficult to learn by yourself. School is a better place to learn the ins and outs of legal research and writing than on the job.

Second, think about getting rid of a second-year requirement. For example, some schools require that you take Constitutional Law, but not necessarily in the first year. If the other choices do not interest you, sign up for a required course now.

Third, pursue a passion. You may not have a legal passion yet. Even if you do, law school has a funny way of beating the passion out of you. (Side note: Don't let it!) If you do have a passion (i.e., environmental law, labor law, entertainment law), or even think you might be passionate about a certain area (i.e., litigation, transactional law), think about using your one elective to fuel (or douse) the flames.

SECOND- AND THIRD-YEAR COURSES

Law school is a lot like joining the military or a cult. In the first year, the powers-that-be (don't ask who the powers-that-be are; just know that they're there) beat you up. Then they indoctrinate you.

(Believe it, you are going to be talking with your law school friends about the fascinating differences between *offensive* non-mutual collateral estoppel and *defensive* non-mutual collateral estoppel. What?) After the indoctrination of the first year, however, the shackles are unhooked, and you're actually free to choose among a bevy of courses. Although most of this book focuses on your first year, here are a few pieces of advice to pull out once you've earned your freedom.

GUIDELINES FOR MAKING CHOICES

1. CHOOSE BY PROFESSOR, NOT TITLE.

Teachers make (or break) law school classes. Tax can be Chinese torture or dim sum—it all depends on the professor.

Law is not easy. Because law is not easy, teaching law (and making the complex understandable) is an art. Only a few professors do it exactly right. The Socratic Method—used by law school professors everywhere—mandates a special blend of question-answer, sometimes (but not always) followed by an explanatory end-of-class lecture. Some professors never get the concoction right. They lecture far too much, question poorly, or maybe just walk up and down the aisle saying nothing. But, as any current law school student will tell you, there's something magical about being in class with a master of the Socratic Method.

Every school has a few professors who excel at the teaching game. You owe it to yourself to find them. One might even change your career path. How many people go to law school intending to be tax lawyers?

2. CONSULT OLDER STUDENTS AND TEACHER EVALUATION GUIDES.

How do you find the best professors and classes? Ask older students. Older students can be an invaluable resource. They can give you old class outlines, old study guides and books, local restaurant tips, and, yes, information about the professors to sign up for and the ones to avoid.

Also, read the teacher evaluation guides. These guides, usually put together by the student association, rate courses and professors on everything from difficulty to effectiveness to teaching style. If your school has one of these guides, use it extensively.

3. TAKE A CLINICAL.

One of the best ways to spice up your schedule and get some valuable real-life experience is to sign up for a clinical. A clinical is essentially working for school credit. The choices are usually varied. For example, you might work for a judge, a public defender, a prosecutor, or legal services (helping those who cannot afford private lawyers). A clinical is especially appropriate for students who do not find legal work in their first summer or perhaps for students who do find legal work, but not in the area in which they want to practice. Employers like real-life experience. You might even end up working for your clinical employer upon graduation. Besides, many students say clinicals are the most fun and most rewarding experiences they have during law school.

4. VARY PAPER AND TEST COURSES.

> *I took four exam classes one semester. I loved not having to write any papers during the term, but come finals week, I was sorry. I had three finals in three days, with little time to recuperate. I should have taken at least one paper class.*
>
> —SHANNON GOTTESMAN, BOSTON COLLEGE LAW SCHOOL

Unlike most college finals, law school finals are tough. You actually have to study for your law school finals—and study hard! Also, law school finals are draining mentally and physically. Too many finals in a row may signal disaster come grade time, especially if you are taking several hard-core courses.

A good mix of paper and exam classes, which usually means about one paper class and three exam classes, is your best bet. During the semester, you can concentrate on your paper. Then, a few weeks before finals, start focusing on your exams.

If you are a procrastinator, be careful. This formula does not work if you are finishing up your paper the night before your big Corporations exam.

5. GET RID OF REQUIREMENTS EARLY.

Most law schools have additional requirements beyond the first year. For example, some schools require Constitutional Law or maybe Corporations. Most states also require that you take a professional responsibility or legal profession course before being admitted to the bar. Don't save these courses for your last semester.

At Harvard Law School a few years ago, third-year students protested, claiming that there were not enough legal profession courses and that many third-years could not graduate without that required course. The school added an additional legal profession course. Don't be put in that position. Figure out what you need for graduation and admittance to the bar, and make sure that you enroll in those courses early on.

6. TAKE IMPORTANT COURSES—EVEN IF THEY ARE NOT MANDATORY.

Even if your school does not require certain courses, most lawyers (and employers) will expect that you have an understanding of certain basic areas of law. Below is a list of important, if not mandatory, courses. You should sign up for all of these classes:

- Administrative Law
- Constitutional Law
- Corporations
- Evidence
- Tax

Here are some other important courses that you might want to consider, although they are not as "basic" as those listed above. If you are definitely not interested, you can skip over these courses. If you think you might be interested, sign up:

- Employment Law or Labor Law
- Federal Courts
- Intellectual Property
- One legal history or legal philosophy (Jurisprudence) class
- Secured Transactions
- Securities Regulation
- Trusts and Estates
- U.C.C. survey course

7. GET OFF THE LAW SCHOOL CAMPUS.

Law school can be all-encompassing. It would be easy to spend every waking moment around other law students and to fill all your course schedules with law school classes. Some law students love law school so much that they want it that way.

For most students, however, law school will represent the end of almost 20 years of formal schooling. Once you start work, you probably will not have time to take a general philosophy course or learn a new language. Most law schools will let you take a small number of select courses at the undergraduate campus or at other graduate schools. If you have an itch for something a little different, scratch it.

8. CONCENTRATE IN AT LEAST ONE AREA OF INTEREST.

During your three years, you should try to take several courses in at least one area that you are passionate about or perhaps want to pursue in terms of a career. Below is a list of several concentrations and the corresponding courses that you may consider. If you are focusing in one of the areas below, you do not have to take all of the corresponding courses, but you should take many of them.

SOME POSSIBLE CONCENTRATIONS AND COURSE GROUPINGS

CIVIL RIGHTS AND CIVIL LIBERTIES

- Constitutional Law*
- Federal Courts*
- Administrative Law*
- Local Government Law
- Discrimination courses, such as Employment Discrimination
- Personal liberties courses, such as Immigration Law
- Economic and social rights courses, such as Poverty Law
- Constitutional theory courses
- Legal history courses, especially those dealing with the Warren Court

CORPORATE LAW

- Corporations*
- Corporate Finance
- Securities Regulation
- Secured Transactions
- Business Planning

- Mergers and Acquisitions
- Corporate Restructuring
- Accounting
- Taxation: Tax and Corporate Tax
- Venture Capital
- Regulatory courses, such as Financial Institutions
- Bankruptcy

CRIMINAL LAW AND PROCEDURE

- Criminal Law*
- Criminal Procedure*
- Evidence*
- Advanced Criminal Procedure
- Juvenile Justice
- Prison Law
- Capital Punishment
- Trial Advocacy
- Clinicals dealing with criminal justice

INTELLECTUAL PROPERTY

- Copyright*
- Intellectual Property*
- Theory of Intellectual Property
- Law of Patent and Trademark

INTERNATIONAL LAW

- International Law
- Transactional Legal Problems
- Conflict of Laws
- International Litigation
- Comparative and Foreign Law
- East Asian Legal Studies
- European Legal Studies
- Islamic Legal Studies
- International Human Rights

JURISPRUDENCE

- Jurisprudence
- Constitutional Jurisprudence
- Critical Race Theory
- Feminist Legal Theory
- Comparative Legal Theory
- Other theory courses

LITIGATION

- Theory of Intellectual Property
- Law of Patent and Trademark

- Administrative Law
- Antitrust Law
- Conflict of Laws
- Copyright and Intellectual Property
- Employment Law
- Employment Discrimination
- Family Law
- Federal Courts
- Immigration Law
- Legal Profession
- Mediation
- Securities Regulation

REGULATORY LAW

- Administrative Law*
- Antitrust Law
- Banking Regulation
- Employment Law
- Environmental Law
- Financial Institutions Regulation
- Food and Drug Law
- Health Care Law
- International Trade
- Labor Law

- Pension Law
- Securities Regulation

TAXATION

- Basic Tax*
- Comparative Tax
- Corporate Tax
- Gift and Estate Tax
- Partnership Tax
- Foreign Tax
- State and Local Taxes

Other Possible Concentrations: Antitrust Law, Constitutional Theory, Cyberspace Law, Employment and Labor Law, Environmental Law, Family Law, Federal Law and Federalism, Financial Institutions, Gender and the Law, Health Law, Law and Economics, Legal History, Legal Profession/Ethics, Legal Services/Poverty Law, Local Government Law, Negotiation, Advanced Property, and Race and Race Relations

* signifies basic courses in each concentration

9. CHECK THE TIME AND DAY.

Are you a morning person? Do you have a boyfriend, girlfriend, or fiancé who you want to spend long weekends with out of state? These are important questions when determining your schedule.

If you know you won't ever make it up for a 7:30 A.M. class, don't sign up for one—it's your money. If being with a loved one on Fridays is more important than a particular law school class, schedule courses that only meet Monday through Thursday. One of the beauties of law school in the second and third years is flexibility.

Also, try to take courses that are reasonably close together during the day. When you have an early morning class and then one in the late afternoon, you may find that you waste most of the time in between, unless you're extremely diligent. If it makes sense, line up your courses as close together as possible without overlapping them.

10. Think about grades—but not too much.

> *I know one student at Harvard who thinks he's a martyr. He takes all the hardest classes and then complains when other students with better grades get the jobs he wants. If his goal was to get those jobs, then he should have accounted for that when he was making his schedule.*
>
> —Greg Gottesman, Harvard Law School

Make no mistake, grades are important for jobs. Don't overburden yourself with too many classes or too many outside activities if such actions will negatively affect your grades. Don't take all your hardest classes in one semester. For example, Tax, Constitutional Law, and Federal Courts are three of the more difficult courses; taking them all in the same semester may spell trouble.

While grades are important, don't make the mistake of concentrating too much on grades. A sincere interest or special training in a particular area (i.e., environmental law) often compensates for average grades in the eyes of some employers. Moreover, just because others do not perform well in certain classes, or find some courses difficult, does not mean that you will, too. Some people have a knack for courses like Tax and others for classes like

Constitutional Law. Your job in law school is to find your own niche. Remember that law school is ultimately a professional school (where you are supposed to be learning a trade), not just another notch for your resume.

—by Greg Gottesman

CHAPTER 6

Law Reviews and Journals

> *I decided from the first day of law school that I would NOT do a journal and have absolutely no regrets about it. I think too many One-Ls freak out about doing law review and too many Three-Ls subsequently regret it. Doing it for the right reasons is great, but doing it for the wrong reasons can be disastrous!*
>
> —MICHAEL CAMUÑEZ, STANFORD LAW SCHOOL

FRIEND OR FOE

Journals (or law reviews) are student-run publications that are home for almost all non-judicial legal scholarship. They are also the biggest enemy and the best friend of law students. Journal work is the major extracurricular activity on almost every law school campus. Journals teach important legal skills and are undoubtedly prestigious. But they are not for everyone. This chapter will lay out the pros and cons of journals and then discuss the law review competition, which is the process you must undertake (usually at the end of your first year) to join most journals.

THE PROS AND CONS OF JOURNALS

What Is Journal Work Like?

Quality—What Editors Do. If you pick up any issue of a law review, you'll probably find a couple of articles written by professors or scholars and perhaps a few shorter pieces by students. The process that leads to publication can be elaborate, requiring considerable time and effort from the journal's members. If you work on a journal, you may get a chance to perform any number of tasks. Journals must acquire articles and essays for publication, so you might be involved in soliciting and reviewing manuscripts. Journals must ensure that their articles are original and meaningful, so you might be involved in research or talking with professors about a proposed manuscript. Journals also tend to do a considerable amount of editing, so you would probably spend a good bit of time grappling with an article's thesis, improving its writing, or checking its citations for substantive and formal accuracy. Law journals also publish pieces written by students, so you might be allowed (or even required) to put your own pen to paper and become a published author. The nature of the work you do as a member of a law journal will vary from student to student and from journal to journal. It all depends on the journal's structure and philosophy, the amount of work that needs to be done, and the number of journal members available to do it.

> *I spend as few as 10 or as many as 40 hours per week on journal work, depending on where we stand in a given process. During the intensive portions of primary editing, the workload is particularly onerous, and nothing can really be done to speed it up. Slogging through the tedium is the only way to get it done. We have very little control over our workload.*
>
> —Richard Myers, Articles Editor,
> *North Carolina Law Review*

Law journals spend a lot of time and effort deciding what to publish. The process for selecting articles generally involves reading submitted manuscripts and evaluating their academic and scholastic worth. One of the greatest ironies of legal journalism is that law professors' ability to be published requires the consent of law *students*. Many editors on law reviews are drawn to the process of selecting pieces for publication. You might enjoy engaging in scholarly discussions about proposed articles and trying to nab the better articles before other journals can get to them. Or you might hate reading long articles, many of which are boring, poorly written, and ultimately rejected. On most law reviews, decisions about publication are made by a committee of members. On some journals, the article selection committee receives input from the journal's body of members. On other journals, the committee is self-sufficient and relatively small. At the *University of Illinois Law Review*, for instance, a four-person committee reviews all submitted articles.

For most members of law reviews, journal work is about *editing*. Editing may take different forms. On many journals, the editors engage the articles and essays on a very high substantive level. Editors might make suggestions for significant changes to the piece's overall structure or thesis. If a journal has a more deferential philosophy toward editing, there will be fewer opportunities for this kind of substantive input. Journals also tend to spend a good deal of time wrestling with an article's prose. Editors ensure, or try to ensure, that the language flows well, that rules of grammar are followed with some fidelity, and that the citations conform with the journal's rules (generally following the *Bluebook*, which contains citation and other grammatical rules for lawyers). Editors often struggle with recalcitrant authors who accuse the journal of cramping their writing style.

An important part of editing on any journal is source-checking. Did you ever notice how many footnotes law journals have citing other sources? Well, the journal has probably verified every single one of those citations at least once (and at least twice on some journals). This can be a tedious process that involves looking up the original sources cited by the author and reading the cited portions to make sure that the citations are correct, both in substance and in form. Most journals rely on their newer members to check sources. Some editors genuinely enjoy this process, although they tend to be in the minority.

Quantity—Time Commitments. Many editors complain that journal work keeps them very busy. They find that they have less time to spend on their classes or with their friends. You may have some control over how much time you spend doing journal work, especially as a third-year student. Because the time commitment on any given journal can be heavy and potentially inflexible, you should definitely get a clear picture of how much work the journal expects from its members *before* you decide to join.

> **TIP:** Some journals give students—particularly One-Ls— the option to work on a discrete editing assignment without insisting on further commitments. Although these assignments (generally citation checking and line editing) tend to be less substantive than other journal work, they can give you an insightful introduction to that particular journal without making a long-term commitment.

At some schools, editors receive academic credit for being a member of the journal. Third-year members of the *Hastings Law Journal*, for instance, receive either one or two units of academic credit, depending on how much work they decide to do. Even if your journal keeps you busy, it may actually help make your class schedule more manageable. Before you decide to join a journal, find out whether you'll be rewarded with academic credit.

Allocation—Who Does What. On most journals, the members are divided into staff members (a.k.a. "editors") and the editorial board (a.k.a. "officers"). Board members tend to have more responsibility and greater input into the institutional decisions of the journal. Board members at some journals tend to do more work than staff members, but not always. The board members are usually selected by the journal's members or its outgoing board members in some kind of election process.

The board member structure can affect your experience on a journal in several ways. First, the ability to work on certain projects or certain types of work may be beyond your control unless you are a board member. Although some journals allow all members to be active in virtually every aspect of the publication process, other journals confine certain activities to a specific committee or group of officers (particularly the selection process for articles). If you think you may be interested in some, but not all, aspects of journal work, it is a good idea to look into how the journal distributes the work and how flexible that system is. Of course, if you enjoy a particular kind of editing and are appointed or elected to the right office, you could get a chance to do what you like for a very long time.

Second, whether you are an officer or a staff member can change your journal experience. By becoming a board member, you may be committing yourself to a heavier and less flexible workload. And while you might find the right niche for yourself, there's always a risk that you'll accept an office that you wind up disliking. (Tip: Board members sometimes receive perks in the form of academic credit or a financial stipend. Being a board member also looks good on a resume.)

A Nice Place to Visit, But I Wouldn't Want to Live There

Before joining a journal, you should get a very clear idea of the scope of the commitment you are making. Be sure to find out how long your membership lasts (or is supposed to last). On the *North Carolina Law Review* and the *Stanford Law Review*, for instance, editors are expected to work on the journal for at least one full academic year. The *Harvard Law Review* demands a two-year commitment from its members. Also, you should know that many journals require their members to do work over the summer.

Skills to Pay the Bills

Many editors on law reviews report that the best part of working on a journal is its educational value. Editors have a chance to be exposed to interesting areas of the law beyond what they learn in the classroom. Their writing and editing skills tend to improve very quickly, as they work intensively writing or improving someone else's writing. Perhaps more importantly, editors on journals find that they learn how to work well with others on long-term projects, an essential skill for lawyers.

> *You learn to work with people. A journal is kind of like an assembly line. What you do affects other people down the line. If there are shortcomings in your work, it's going to be a burden on the next person.*
>
> —MARC WILLIAMS, NOTES EDITOR, *Southern California Law Review*

Not everyone finds the training useful. Some editors find editing tedious and obscure. They complain that too much time is spent analyzing useless citation rules. Law review work can be a great educational experience, but it's not for everyone.

Resume Power

One of the most popular reasons for joining a law review is that it serves as a valuable credential in applying for jobs or clerkships. Employers and especially judges place some value on the sorts of writing and editing skills that journal work tends to nurture. Quality research and writing are an important part of many lawyers' work, especially in litigation. And your colleagues will probably often ask you to help edit early drafts of motions, briefs, and other legal documents.

Additionally, membership on the school's law review or other journals is often competitive and prestigious. *The Cornell Law Review*, for example, selected 42 members from a pool of 275 applicants in 1995. As such, the journal's name might make your resume look a little more impressive, in terms of raw prestige. Again, this can be particularly true if you become a board member or officer of your journal. The words "President" or "Editor-in-Chief" definitely add a lot to a student's resume.

Of course, it is important not to overestimate that prestige value. Other factors, such as grades, will always factor into a judge's or employer's decision to extend an offer.

> *The Articles Editor position was helpful in landing my clerkship. My judge asked about it during the interview. I anticipate long-term career benefits from having served on the board, particularly if I ever apply for a teaching position. As to whether those expectations will be met, the jury is still out.*
>
> —RICHARD MYERS, ARTICLES EDITOR, *North Carolina Law Review*

Writing Opportunities

Most law journals afford their members the opportunity to write short academic commentaries for publication. These "Notes" or "Comments" vary greatly in size and content. Some comments are five pages; others are 50 pages. Some summarize and analyze a particular case or statute; others explore whole bodies of law.

For many law school students, the opportunity to write for publication is one of the most significant benefits of being on a journal. The writing process is often both educational and rewarding. A published comment can also add a nice line to your resume. And many law schools allow students to fulfill their school's writing requirement or receive academic credit for writing on a journal. The writing process can also be frustrating and time-consuming. Students can underestimate the difficulty of selecting a topic, developing a meaningful and original thesis, and of surviving their journal's editing process. Many students admit that they are somewhat disappointed with their final product, although few claim to *regret* writing in the first place.

> *One of the best things about writing a Note is that you learn how to finish a big project. You have to compromise a little; I don't think your Note is ever what you want it to be. You learn how to set it aside and call it "done." I think that's a very important skill, especially if you want to be a professor or continue writing.*
>
> —Marc Williams, Notes Editor, *Southern California Law Review*

Different journals have different approaches toward student writing. First, the question of *whether* you get to be published is answered in different ways. On most journals, members submit completed drafts to a committee on the journal that decides which pieces will be published. At some schools, such as Boalt and the University of North Carolina, all members are *required* to write a lengthy Note, which then goes to a committee that approves or rejects the piece for publication. Some journals actually *guarantee* their members the opportunity to write for publication, assuming the author is able to meet the writing schedule and certain standards of quality.

Second, the writing process itself can be very different from journal to journal. Some journals take a very hands-on approach to student writing—assigning the particular topics to authors, providing lots of input into early drafts, and requiring heavy editing. Other journals take a more hands-off approach, allowing students to select their own topics and providing less substantive input (or at least fewer mandatory suggestions) throughout the editing process. Most journals are somewhere in between.

If you're considering joining a journal, and you fancy yourself a scribe, be sure to find out in advance how the journal handles student writing.

Socializing on Journals

Like any extracurricular activity, law journals can be a forum for meeting and interacting with interesting people. Law review editors often work closely with each other over long periods of time and form strong friendships that last beyond law school. Also, much of journal work is a team effort: Big decisions are made by committees or votes of the membership, article selection involves discussion and debate, and editing a large article will require the combined efforts of several (sometimes dozens) editors. Editors on closely knit journals often feel some bond with their fellow editors.

> *The best part of working on the journal is the quality of the people I am working closely with this year. I honestly anticipate that the friendships I have made on the board will be some of my longest-lasting professional friendships.*
>
> —RICHARD MYERS, ARTICLES EDITOR, *North Carolina Law Review*

Of course, that sort of experience varies from school to school, from journal to journal, and from member to member. An Article Notes Editor on a newly formed law journal complained about the lack of interaction among journal members: "People just walk into the office, get their work done, and leave. For the most part, I never know what other people are working on, and no one else knows what I'm working on." Such impressions tend to be in the minority. Nonetheless, it's a good idea to ask current members about their impressions of the journal's social climate.

> **TIP:** Working on a law journal can demand a lot of time and effort from you and might stifle your social life. Many members of law review find it difficult to manage journal work while taking classes and maintaining a social life. Truth be told, sometimes classes are the first sacrifice.

Other Perks—Credit and Money

The amount of academic credit may vary from journal to journal and even from student to student. For instance, the amount of credit may depend on how much work you do (*Hastings Law Journal*), on whether you are a board member (*University of Pennsylvania Law Review*), or on whether you write something for publication (*Columbia Law Review*). Many schools, of course, give no academic credit at all for law journal membership. And there appears to be a trend toward limiting or eliminating such credit. (Duke Law School recently stopped giving academic credit to journal members. Boalt Hall recently reduced the academic credit that journal members received.)

Members of some journals (such as the *Texas Law Review* and the *Iowa Law Review*) receive a financial stipend. And some law schools provide other financial incentives for journal work. Vanderbilt Law School, for instance, gives financial writing prizes for the best student Note or Comment written for publication. For the most part, however, financial rewards are extremely rare, and often only certain officers/board members are eligible. Usually, there is no combat pay for fighting in the front lines of legal journalism.

WHICH JOURNAL SHOULD I JOIN?

Many law schools have more than one journal. Most law schools will tend to have one "official" journal (such as the *Yale Law Journal* or the *Texas Law Review*) and any number of "specialized" journals (such as the *Yale Law and Policy Review* or the *Texas International Law Journal*). In choosing which journal to join, you should take a careful look at the factors listed above. Some students choose to become members of more than one journal.

Membership on the law school's "official" journal will tend to be more competitive and more prestigious, although this is not always the case. The school's "specialized" journals, as the name implies, will tend to focus on a particular topic or set of topics in legal academia.

Some journals may be associated with a particular political stance, and in some cases, the reputation a journal carries is very strong. Unfortunately, your fellow students, or even prospective employers, may presume that your political orientation aligns with the journal. When you join a journal, make sure that you aren't unwittingly branding yourself with an ideology that you don't share.

THE LAW REVIEW COMPETITION

If you want to become a member of your school's law journal, chances are that you'll experience something called "the writing competition." This painful device, descended from medieval trial-by-torture, is the dominant selection method for most of the "official" law reviews and plays at least some role in the selection process for nearly all journals. Grades, personal statements, and affirmative action also may factor into the selection of new editors.

WHAT IS THE WRITING COMPETITION?

The "writing competition" means something different at each school. The general idea is to test your writing and/or editing skills by having you compose a writing or editing sample in a fairly short amount of time. Your school's writing competition, for instance, might give you a court opinion and ask you to summarize and analyze it, or it might present you with a legal problem and ask you to comment on it. Some journals also might provide you with an already written article or commentary and ask you to edit it, although this practice is less common. The journal may give you anywhere from three days to two weeks, and it's almost certainly going to be an endurance test.

PREPARING FOR THE WRITING COMPETITION

The first year of law school is meant to develop your ability to think like a lawyer. Unfortunately, it tends to do little to help you *write* like one. The writing competition might be your first major writing project since college. If that's the case, you should try to avoid a cold start.

Most journals are fairly open and honest about their writing competition. They will probably provide you with some (if not a lot of) information about the process. Here are some tips for maximizing your preparedness for the competition:

1. Look for free advice.

At some schools, the law review (or other student organizations) will give you tips on how to take the competition and how to compose a good writing sample. The journal might hold a meeting for interested applicants or may simply put out a memo or e-mail to One-Ls. It is more than acceptable to call the law review well before the competition to ask if, when, and how such information will be made available.

2. Obtain and practice using previous competitions.

Try to get a look at some of the competitions from previous years. You might be able to get these from second- or third-year classmates, or from the law journal itself. Again, a phone call to the journal is a good place to start.

3. Find out what counts and what doesn't.

The writing competition is meant to test writing and/or editing skills in general, but the specific skills being targeted may vary from journal to journal. It is important to focus on things that actually earn you points and to avoid distractions. For instance, some journals may tell their graders to disregard spelling errors, while others instruct their graders to take off points for such mistakes. What counts is not always intuitive. For instance, the Harvard Law Review, which publishes the Bluebook, does not test bluebooking on its writing competition!

4. Go through a dry run.

This may be very time-consuming, but well worth it. If you can get your hands on a previous year's competition, set a few hours aside to go through a dry run. Don't actually produce a final product unless you have a lot of time on your hands. (Shouldn't you be studying?) But constructing a rough outline of what you would write will give you some insight into what's involved in the process and how fast you'll have to work.

5. Read the law review.

A law journal can have its own writing style. Pick up a copy of the journal you're applying to and thumb through it. Try to get a sense of how formal legal writing tends to be in that journal. Chances are, the graders will reward those who write like they do.

6. Improve your writing skills.

Improving basic writing skills, even after college, is easier than many people think. For instance, The Elements of Style by William Strunk Jr. and E. B. White is a very short and insightful guide to English usage. If you have never read it, do so before the competition. You may be surprised how a few simple pieces of advice can help you write more clearly and more persuasively.

DURING THE WRITING COMPETITION

1. READ THE INSTRUCTIONS FIRST.

> *There was a requirement that we needed to staple our entries to manila folders, with the text on one side and the footnotes on the other. On the day I had to mail in the competition, I didn't have the folders. I was in Brooklyn on a Jewish holiday, and all the stationery stores were closed. I had no idea what to do.*
>
> —MARC WILLIAMS, NOTES EDITOR, *Southern California Law Review*

Don't lose out because you didn't follow the rules. The law review may require you to produce your writing sample in very specific formatting (font type/size, margins, and so on) or to abide by strict page lengths. Or it may require you to turn in a certain number of copies. Or it may require you to turn your work in at a different place from where you picked it up. Or there may be substantive requirements on how many sources you can/should/must cite. In short, the competition may have any number of obscure, technical requirements that can cost you big points or last-minute panic if you don't read the instructions carefully at the beginning of the process.

> **TIP:**   The technical instructions for the writing competition will probably be the same from year to year. If the law review provides examples of previous competitions, you

can read the instructions from previous years and get a preview of things to come. But also read the instructions that come with the actual competition.

2. ORGANIZE YOUR MATERIALS.

The writing competition itself will probably consist of a whole lot of paper. Most journals will provide you with all the research materials you need to complete the writing sample (although a few will have you do your own research). Have a couple of heavy-duty three-ring binders and your three-hole puncher ready on the first day of the competition. Or, if you are willing to spend a few bucks, go to a copy center as soon as you pick up all the materials and get the packet bound. Keeping the materials in order can avoid the chaos of a random heap of papers, as well as the crisis of lost materials.

3. FIND A BUDDY.

The writing competition is bound to be a strain. Chances are, you'll have just finished your exams (not to mention the hardest year of law school), classmates will have already started their summer jobs and/or vacations, the weather will be nice, and all the temptations of procrastination will be magnified exponentially. A good strategy for surviving the writing competition is the "buddy system."

Find a friend who's also taking the competition and make a pact. Agree to call each other in the morning to make sure the other is up and working. Agree to take short breaks when necessary. Make sure the other isn't forgetting to do important things like eating and sleeping. In short, team up against the enemies—procrastination, stress, and exhaustion. The law review competition can be a nightmare, but like any nightmare, it's easier to get through with someone else.

> **TIP:** The law review competition will probably forbid collaboration. Make sure that you and your buddy avoid talking about the substance of the competition.

4. BEING A PRODIGY CAN BE PRODIGAL; JUST PRODUCE!

Pick your argument, describe it clearly, stick to it, and don't be tangential. Believe it or not, the most common complaint from people who grade competitions is that the sample didn't have a thesis! The author probably thought there was a thesis, but obscured it by trying to do too much (and inevitably doing nothing at all).

In general, your goal should be to produce a writing sample that is well-reasoned, well-supported, and well-written. By the time you've finished your One-L year, you'll be thinking like a lawyer (at least, that's what John Houseman playing Professor Kingsfield promised his class in the beginning of The Paper Chase). You will already possess the skills of argument and persuasion that will earn you big points on the writing competition. When doing the competition, stick to a specific and clearly defined argument or line of analysis that you can support well. If your argument happens to be pure brilliance, that's great. But don't try to make your argument creative or original at the expense of clarity and support. A boring argument that works is better than a creative one that doesn't.

> *Focus on one thing. You have to understand the weaknesses of your argument, but you don't have to take a balanced approach or throw out every possible argument for the other side. It's not like a law school exam.*
>
> —MARC WILLIAMS, NOTES EDITOR, *Southern California Law Review*

5. REMEMBER YOUR AUDIENCE.

Guess who usually grades the law review competition—the current editors, who happen to be law students, just like you. Knowing that students will be grading your competition should give you some insight into how to write and/or edit. Don't assume the reader knows arcane details about the law. In fact, don't assume that the grader knows much more about the law than you do. If you are annoyed by something you are writing, the grader probably will be, too. If you think what you are writing is great, there's a good chance the grader will, too.

When writing, consider that the grader may be reading your competition along with 40 others. The grader also may be doing it during the summer when time is scarce, especially if the grader is working for a big law firm. Clear writing and editing is rewarded handsomely. So is well-placed humor, but only *good* humor. Be careful. There is nothing worse than reading the work of someone who is trying to be funny . . . unsuccessfully.

6. SET ASIDE TIME FOR PROOFREADING—YES, REALLY!

Many (if not most) students who take the writing competition complain that they never had time to thoroughly proofread their submission. Running out of time is understandable, but also avoidable. Don't put off the proofreading stage until the very last minute—or, worse, until after the competition is over. At some point, you need to accept that the piece is essentially finished and start to fine-tune it. Decide ahead of time what that point will be and stick to it. It will be tempting to continue struggling with your argument, reading new materials, or looking for new angles. But these efforts will tend to be less and less fruitful as time goes by. And the perils of punctuation mistakes are more serious than you might think.

On some journals' writing competitions, graders are instructed to take points off if an applicant makes a clear grammatical or spelling error. More importantly, if basic errors persist, then you're going to be hurt, no matter what the journal's policies. In any written work, errors will always undercut the author's credibility and give the readers less confidence in the document in front of them. Also, remember that a grader who has to read dozens of submissions may be more likely to notice typos and misspellings than substantive flaws. The lesson is not that you should sacrifice substance for form, but that you should allocate enough time to attend to the needs of both substance and form.

7. Turn it in.

Even if you don't have time to "finish" the writing competition, you should always turn in what you have done. There's absolutely no cost to handing in a partially finished competition, when the alternative is to give yourself an automatic zero. After all, you wouldn't refuse to turn in an exam just because you ran out of time. No one's writing competition is perfect. Yours won't be either. If you want to work on a journal, give yourself a shot—almost everyone who is on a journal is surprised to have made it.

—by Kimo Peluso

CHAPTER 7

Extracurricular Activities and Moot Court

BEYOND THE CLASSROOM

The title of this chapter will undoubtedly make many future first-year law students laugh. Extracurricular activities? Who has time for that when you're eating, sleeping, and breathing Civil Procedure? Moot court competitions? Who has time for them when you're practically dating the Criminal Law textbook? The truth, however, is that extracurricular activities are an important part of the first-year law student experience. Participating in activities outside of normal classwork provides you with excellent practical knowledge, a well-rounded resume, and often the social outlet you need to counteract the stress of first-year classes.

STUDENT ORGANIZATIONS

JUST WHO ARE THESE PEOPLE?

Most student organizations are run by second- and third-year law students. These organizations draw their membership from students in all three years.

WHAT ARE THESE GROUPS, ANYWAY?

Student organizations come in a variety of types. They are all similar in that the participants are usually motivated individuals who are interested in a particular field or activity. The following is a list of several types of student organizations found at law schools across the country. Moot court and other law school competitions will be discussed later in the chapter.

Journals. Working on a journal is probably the most common extracurricular activity. The pros and cons of working on a journal are discussed in detail in the previous chapter.

Political Groups. Many student groups are associated with political organizations and sponsor activities in their law schools on behalf of those organizations. These groups might include the Democratic Law Student Association, Republican Law Student Association, and Libertarian Law Students. Often these groups are active during specific political campaigns.

Legal Aid Groups. Many student groups advocate helping individuals who do not have access to legal assistance. These organizations might include Law Students for Prisoners' Rights, Legal Aid for Immigrants, and Public Defender societies.

> *I joined the Harvard Defenders my first year. It was my first chance to see what it felt like to be a real lawyer with real clients. I had a client who had stolen about $100 from a store where he was employed. He was sure he was going to jail. I talked with the magistrate on my client's behalf. We worked out a deal where my client would pay back the money but serve no time. The smile on my client's face is one of the things I will remember most about my first year in law school.*
>
> —Greg Gottesman, Harvard Law School

National Legal Associations. Many groups represent a national legal organization on the student level. These groups are often organized by alumni of the law school. Such groups might include the Law School Civil Rights and Civil Liberties Union.

Religious Groups. These groups draw members according to their interest in a particular religion. These organizations might include the Christian Legal Society and Jewish Law Students Association.

Issue Groups. Another type of student organization revolves around important issues, usually of a legal nature. An example of this type of group is Law Students Against the Death Penalty.

Cultural and Ethnic Groups. Many student organizations promote the advancement of a particular cultural or ethnic group. These groups might include the Black Law Student Association and South Asian Law Students Association.

Lifestyle Groups. Some groups on campus promote alternative lifestyles, such as the Gay and Lesbian Law Student Association. Other organizations cater to those students with children. Some groups are formed not for law students, but for the partners of law students.

Awareness Groups. Many student groups revolve around increasing community awareness about a particular issue. These groups might include the Women's Law Association and the Environmental Law Society.

Athletic Groups. For those law students who prefer the challenge of scoring 23 points a game over the intricacies of Federal Rule of Civil Procedure 23, many schools offer athletic groups devoted to your usual variety of activities: basketball, football, softball, and so on. Many students find athletic activities an excellent way to counterbalance the academic rigors of student life and to relieve some stress.

> *Participating in the Student Lawyer Athletic Program (SLAP) at my school was rewarding in many ways. First, it was a great release from the pressures of the first year of law school when 15 of my sectionmates would go straight from Civil Procedure to the football field to take on our friends from other sections. Second, being the commissioner of the league was beneficial in interviewing. The league always came up, and law firms are always looking for a good shortstop for their softball team.*
>
> —DAVID SHAW, NEW YORK UNIVERSITY LAW SCHOOL

Law School Parody. And, finally, for the frustrated actors and singers out there, there is the performing showcase that is often called Law Revue or the Parody. The show, which is usually quite humorous, offers talented students the opportunity to send off their professors, deans, and assorted law school characters in grand fashion. Although seemingly time-consuming and apparently requiring some skill, the people in the Parody always seem to be having the most fun.

> *The best move I made was auditioning for the Law Revue—our two-and-a-half hour musical law school Parody. I met second- and third-years who gave me perspective on first-year angst (not to mention their old outlines). After spending 20 hours a week in rehearsal, my grades actually improved. And when else would I have been able to belt out a tune in the spotlight with a 17-piece orchestra just three blocks from Broadway!*
>
> —MELISSA MORGAN, NEW YORK UNIVERSITY LAW SCHOOL

WHERE CAN I FIND INFORMATION?

Student organizations gain members through a variety of ways. At some schools, special sign-up days for first-year students are planned, and students have the opportunity to put their names on mailing lists. Other schools don't plan sign-up days, and student groups solicit potential members by posting information around the school, or by depositing information in the mailboxes of all first-years. A number of schools have moved into the 1990s; information on their student organizations can be accessed over the Internet. This is especially useful for entering first-years who are unsure if a particular group exists at their future school, or want to find out which groups are available to them.

WILL I HAVE TIME TO DO THESE ACTIVITIES?

Perhaps the most difficult question to answer is whether first-years will have any time to engage in activities outside their required studies. The answer is a resounding yes. As the saying goes, "All work and no extracurriculars makes Jack a dull student." Or something like that.

The truth is that no one will force you to participate in student organizations. Some students are more than happy to bury themselves in their reading, requiring a minimum of human interaction. But generally speaking, those students who do engage in extracurricular activities add to the depth of their experience at law school. And here's a little piece of news: Those second- and third-years—the ones who are running the majority of student organizations—were once first-year students, too! That's right, they were once sweating it out, thrust into a new academic environment with hours upon hours of reading. So they know the plight of first-years, and they usually will not make excessive demands on the time of first-years. If they did, they would quickly find their membership dwindling, and their clubs would mysteriously dry up. So don't lose heart; there should be time for everything.

WHY BOTHER?

The decision to participate in a student organization is a personal one that rests with the individual student. Most law school students, however, participate in at least one student organization, and most would say they benefited from the experience.

> *Each time I check my mailbox at school, I am reminded that extracurricular life is alive and well. Coming from a women's college, I was particularly pleased to find a strong women's community at my school, reflected in the mentoring programs sponsored by Law Women, the strategy sessions led by the 2X Task Force to discuss legal education reform, and the outreach efforts of the Battered Women's Project. My school is also a great cultivating ground for new student ideas. For instance, working with faculty of the NYU Global Law School Program, we started a student exchange project with law students from Humboldt University in Berlin, Germany. I think it is this strong student involvement, particularly in public interest activities, that really contributes to making law school a humane and friendly place.*
>
> —LAUREN ASTE, NEW YORK UNIVERSITY LAW SCHOOL

Aside from the numerous social benefits that have been described in this chapter, the fact remains that one place where student organizations always look good is on a resume. If an important goal of the law school experience is to get a job as a lawyer, it is not unreasonable to say that involvement in student organizations is a factor that contributes to that goal. Whether involvement in student activities provides a comfortable topic to discuss in a law firm interview or allows a student to meet practitioners in their area of interest, participation in student organizations demonstrates the desire of a student to go beyond the pages of textbooks and the four walls of the classroom.

MOOT COURT AND OTHER COMPETITIONS

> *Imagine standing all alone behind a podium, knees shaking as you stare into the eyes of four judges. As your 15 minutes quickly pass, the judges try desperately to stump you with their questions and to scare you into giving up your dream of becoming a star litigator. Despite their sometimes challenging (yet sometimes stupid) questions and hypotheticals, you remain calm and respond with confidence. After some deliberation, the judges announce a decision in favor of your client, and although you are arguing in a classroom instead of a courtroom and competing in moot court rather than in real court, the taste of success is just as sweet.*
>
> —MICHELLE WILCK, NEW YORK UNIVERSITY LAW SCHOOL

The reason this section is called "Moot Court and Other Competitions" is not to downplay the significance of other competitions. Many law schools have programs where first-years can compete in a variety of settings. One of the most significant of these other competitions is mock trial. In mock trial, law students are assigned to one side of a civil or criminal case and actually question mock witnesses in front of a student jury and a judge. Another major event in some law schools is the negotiation competition. In that competition, students are given conflicting clients with different interests. After the students negotiate against each other, judges score the teams or individual students based on a variety of parameters, such as style, preparation, technique, and so on. Students with the highest scores move on to the next round. Other competitions include client counseling and essay writing. These other competitions, however, are usually not as extensive as the moot court competitions offered in law schools nationwide.

MOOT COURT

The term "moot court" is derived from the term "moot," which is defined as follows: "to argue a case at law (as a hypothetical case) as a student in a law school." Moot court competitions are, simply put, re-creations of arguments that take place in appellate courts. Competitions can last anywhere from a single day to an entire school year and provide what many law students describe as the most intellectually challenging activity of their law school careers. Before discussing the ins and outs of moot court competitions, let's look at the step-by-step process involved.

Step 1 Receiving the Record

A moot court competition begins with either one or two students receiving a copy of a record around which the moot court competition will revolve. The record consists of a fictitious fact pattern, much like the factual record one would receive from a real trial court. The record contains documents relating to a legal action brought by one party against another party, and the students will be told which side they represent. In addition to factual material about the substance of the suit, the record will usually contain a motion for summary judgment or motion to dismiss filed by the defending party, as well as a motion to deny the first motion filed by the party who brought the original action.

As mentioned earlier, a moot court competition is a re-creation of an appellate argument. While trial advocacy competitions re-create a courtroom setting, moot court competitions simulate how an argument would be put forth in an appellate court. Therefore, for a case to be tried before an appellate court, there has to have been some decision at the district court level for the loser to appeal. The record may also contain a decision from an intermediate appellate court. The final part of the record usually contains the motion to appeal filed by the losing side, along with an order granting the appeal from the appropriate appellate court. The record will usually end with this grant of appeal, listing the specific issues to be addressed. These one or two issues are the issues that the competitors will argue.   .

Step 2   Writing the Brief

After receiving the record, the competitors will usually receive a packet of information regarding the brief. The brief is the competitors' written argument to the appellate court laying out the appropriate facts and law in support of their side of the argument. Over the course of law students' careers, most will write several briefs, and there are a host of books devoted to the art of brief writing. For our purposes, it is enough to say that the writing of the brief is the second step of the process. The competitors will research the legal issues presented in the record and explain why their side should win. Most moot court competitions supply competitors with a list of guidelines covering the technical requirements of the brief, including page limits, font sizes, section names, and heading labels.

Different moot court competitions vary in the emphasis placed on the brief in relation to the competitors' scores in the competition. Whether the brief is weighted heavily or not, it is of primary importance in laying the foundation for the next phase of the moot court competition: oral argument.

Step 3   Making the Oral Argument

Okay, here's where it gets interesting. For those students looking for the "competition" part of moot court, look no further. During oral arguments, the two sides (the side bringing the appeal, called the *petitioner* or *appellant*, and the side defending against the appeal, called the *respondent* or *appellee*) argue against each other on the certified issues in front of a panel of anywhere from two to nine judges.

The formalities involved in moot court competitions are extensive. Each judge is given a grading sheet listing categories under which the student's oral presentation should be analyzed. These categories can include: persuasiveness, technique, quality of argument, knowledge of the law, and confidence of the arguer. Oral arguments usually begin with the petitioner coming to a podium and beginning the presentation to the court. The judges will then ask the petitioner questions regarding the law and facts in the argument presented. Panels are usually described in terms of temperature: If there is a *cold bench*, the panelists ask very few questions, and you are left quoting large parts of your argument to the panel; if there is a *hot bench*, the questions are coming at you like wildfire, and you barely have time to breathe. The length of the petitioner's argument is usually 15 minutes, after which the respondent comes to the podium and is subject to questioning for the same length of time. When the respondent is finished, the petitioner may come back to the podium, usually for one to three minutes. This period, called *rebuttal*, allows the petitioner to get the last word on any issues of concern to the panel.

Competitors know how much time they have remaining by looking at time cards flashed at them by a clerk of the court. At the end of all the oral arguments, the panel usually sends the competitors out of the room, allowing the judges to complete their grading forms for each of the participants. After several minutes, the competitors are brought back into the room, where the judges inform them which side won and critique their oral arguments.

These three elements appear in all moot court competitions held in law schools across the country. There are variations among the competitions: Some are set in an appeals court, some in a supreme court; some allow two competitors per side, some allow three. But the three elements listed above are fairly standard in every moot court competition you will encounter.

WHEN WOULD I GET INVOLVED IN MOOT COURT?

Some schools have moot court boards. Like the student organizations described earlier, moot court boards usually draw their membership from students in all three years of law school. Typically, first-year students will engage in some sort of competition in order to be considered for a spot on a moot court board. Many schools tie first-year moot court competitions into a lawyering or legal research and writing class, where students are instructed on the mechanics of brief writing and oral argument by third-years and practicing attorneys.

First-year competitions allow students to get a taste of what moot court involves and are often the first opportunity students have to engage in public speaking in a law school setting. Performing well in an oral argument, however, is not the only way students are accepted into moot court organizations. Often, moot court boards will have a writing competition, selecting members from the first-year class who demonstrate superior brief-writing skills.

Moreover, oral arguments in moot court are only half the story. Many moot court boards produce an annual *casebook*. Casebooks contain moot court problems written by law students and involve tremendous amounts of preparation. Students who write casebook problems have thoroughly researched an area of the law on which there is a dispute among courts, and they write this dispute into an elaborate problem to be argued by moot court competitors. Moot court boards that produce casebooks of high quality will usually find a demand for their casebooks across the country for use in moot court competitions at various law schools. The creativity required of the oral advocate in a moot court competition finds a parallel in the creativity required to write a successful moot court problem.

WHY MOOT COURT?

> As a first-year, I applied to NYU's Moot Court Board
> without a complete understanding of what the
> Board was all about. Having served on the Board
> for two years, I now realize the extraordinary
> benefits of joining a moot court board or other
> journal-type organization during law school. First,
> these organizations are great social outlets. Second,
> they provide opportunities for students to sharpen
> their legal research, writing, and/or oral advocacy
> skills by writing and/or arguing on current legal
> issues, usually of the student's choice. This effort
> may even result in publication of the student's
> work. Third, participation in these organizations
> helps to break up the monotony of the classroom
> experience. Finally, employers are generally
> impressed with student involvement in these
> organizations, and students can converse about
> their experiences during job interviews.
>
> —JEFFREY GLICKMAN, NEW YORK UNIVERSITY LAW SCHOOL

Some opinion surveys have shown that the fear of public speaking
has been ranked higher than the fear of death. Indeed, the thought
of standing in front of three accomplished attorneys/professors/
judges and being interrogated for 15 minutes on a complex area of
law is enough to send anyone running straight into the library to
read three hours of torts and feel grateful. Yet, the truth is that
moot court competitions develop distinct skills in individuals who
compete in them, skills they may not be able to acquire in any other
activity in law school.

The first skill developed during the course of a moot court
competition is the ability to write a brief. Whether one intends to

be a litigator and write briefs for a living or to work primarily on transactions and write only when necessary, the ability to perform competent research and successfully convey a written message is a valuable skill in every area of the law.

The second skill developed in a moot court competition is, of course, the ability to argue. Now, we're not talking about the run-of-the-mill, give-me-the-remote-so-I-can-change-to-football argue, either. The arguing we are referring to is the kind that takes place in an appellate court. It is a unique kind of arguing: you are given a limited factual pattern, and you are forced to develop a familiarity with a broad array of case law. Yet, this skill of presenting complex arguments and presenting them well is one that a seasoned moot court competitor will take with him or her into every future public speaking engagement.

> *In my second year of law school, I took Federal Income Tax and also competed in my school's moot court competition. While I now have only a hazy recollection of the federal tax code, I can definitively cite you at least 10 cases I relied on when I argued in the competition finals. The experience of arguing in moot court competitions is one of the most intellectually exciting experiences at law school. While it may be difficult, daunting, and at times downright scary, you should definitely take advantage of the unique opportunities offered by a moot court competition.*
>
> —RICHARD S. LOBEL, NEW YORK UNIVERSITY LAW SCHOOL

BEYOND FIRST-YEAR COMPETITIONS

The purpose of most moot court boards goes beyond sponsoring competitions for first-years and producing casebooks. Moot court boards also run competitions for competitors from their school or from schools across the country.

> *As a second-year student on the moot court board, I represented my law school at the largest moot court competition in the country. It was an exciting weekend, for after writing a 40-page brief and practicing over 25 oral arguments, my teammate and I were finally ready to put all of our hard work to the test. Although we did not come in first place (or tenth place for that matter), it was still a wonderful and memorable weekend.*
>
> —MICHELLE WILCK, NEW YORK UNIVERSITY LAW SCHOOL

While there may be a number of first-years who do not make it onto a moot court board their first year, they should not be discouraged. The in-school competitions sponsored by moot court boards allow a large number of students to participate and are often quite prestigious competitions, with final rounds judged by district court judges, appeals court judges, and even Supreme Court justices. For moot court board members, there will usually be opportunities to compete in national competitions on a variety of legal topics. The bottom line is that participation in moot court is something that any legal practitioner will look upon favorably; it has been compared with journal experience as one of the most important factors potential legal employers examine. But regardless of how it may help you in the occupational setting, moot court experience will likely add to the quality of your experience at law school and hopefully beyond as well.

—by Richard S. Lobel

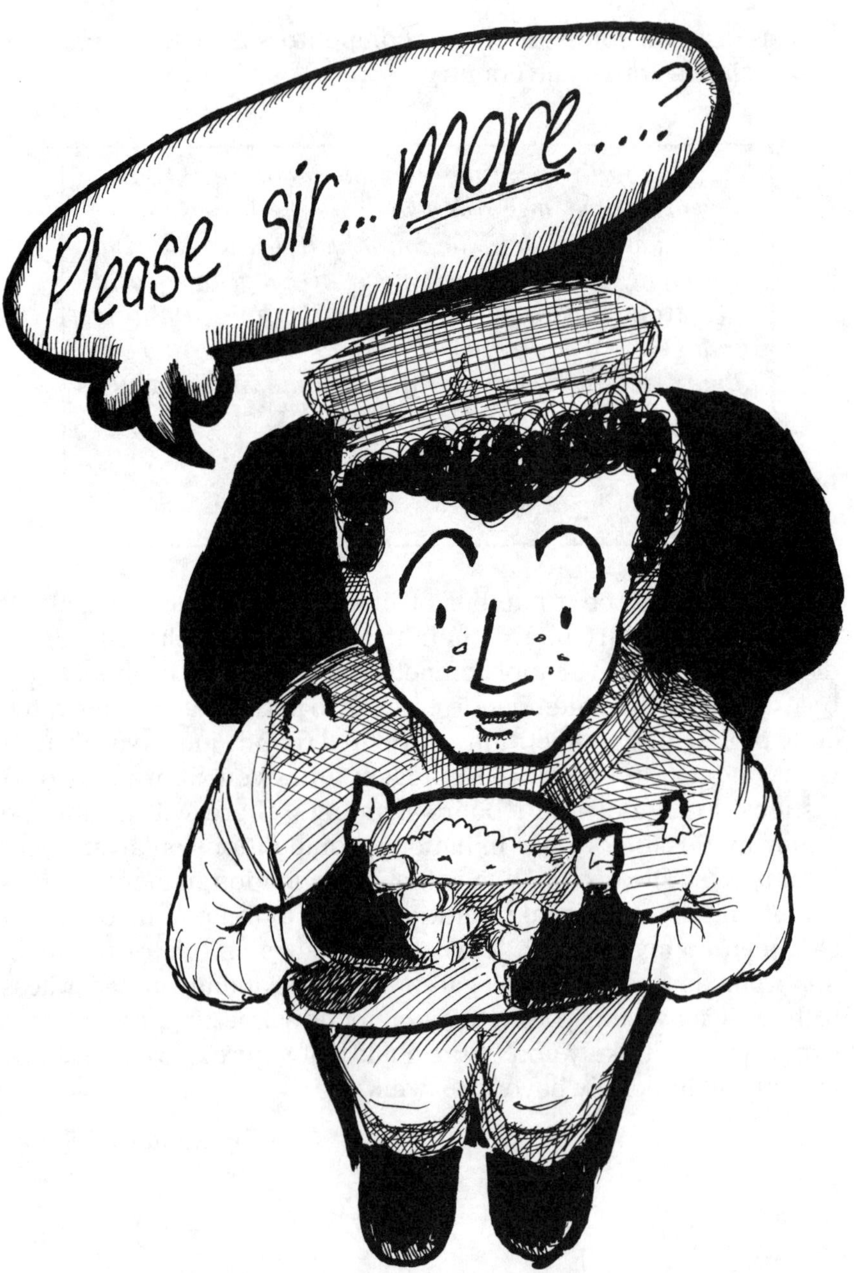
Please sir... more...?

CHAPTER 8

Financial Aid

PAYING FOR LAW SCHOOL

Welcome to law school. Now cough up the cash, please. Just because a school has lecture halls, libraries, and a rare book collection, all of which bestow an aura of a hallowed sanctum of learning, does not mean that it hovers outside the sphere of financial reality. Schools are constantly finding new ways to bring in money to support the law school program. Often, these forms of assistance come through alumni support, fundraisers, and even bake sales (which can be quite tasty). Primarily, though, the vein through which a school sucks its fiscal blood is the age-old method known in academia as "Bleeding the Student Dry." And this method is quite effective.

Oh, yes, to get your chance to pull in the hefty bucks as a high falootin' big firm attorney, defending asbestos manufacturers and those harmless tobacco companies, you must pay, and pay dearly. Before you are granted that shiny J.D. at the end of three years of that nonstop joyride we here refer to as law school, it will be your school's job to make sure that you feel the financial impact of that privilege.

Invariably on the page of the school's brochure where tuition is discussed there will be pictures of very attractive male and female law students with quotes stating how they "love the community" of the school and "enjoy the challenge" that the study of law brings.

These photo layouts of attractive people are actually products of years of joint hard work from a New York ad firm and a psychological research firm that are designed specifically to distract you from the fact that when the brochure says "$11,000," it's not "per year"—it's "per semester."

Also not included in the glossy brochure is that it is not uncommon for tuition to "automatically" increase at the rate of 5 percent per year. While 5 percent might not seem like much if you are buying a classic Vanilla Ice album or a commercial outline for your Contracts exam, 5 percent of $22,000 is more than $1,000. It might be a good idea to ask the financial aid office at your school what the traditional rate of increase of tuition is per year. If the office claims that it varies from year to year and you cannot get a straight answer, do a little research and check out tuition costs for the past five or so years to get a good idea of previous rate increases.

Speaking of financial aid, the first thing you need to do is find out where the financial aid office is located at your school. Generally, it will be near the administrative offices. If you happen to walk into a room filled with tons of paper and tape, you haven't stumbled into a supply room: Congratulations, you've found the financial aid office! Overflowing with red tape and forms in triplicate, quadruplicate, and quintuplicate, the financial aid office is the nerve center of all things concerning how you will finance your law school education. At its best, the financial aid office is a fruitful resource center and efficient document-processing center. You will be able to get information on your financial aid status and process your stacks of financial documents at the same time. At its worst, the financial aid office is a burgeoning jungle of bureaucracy, misinformation, delays, lost forms, and frustration. More often than not, though, the financial aid experience only becomes a nightmare when a student has broken one of the four cardinal rules of financial aid.

THE CARDINAL RULES OF FINANCIAL AID (FROM LEAST IMPORTANT TO MOST)

1. DON'T PISS OFF YOUR FINANCIAL AID OFFICE.

Most law schools do not allot many staff members to man the financial aid office. As a result, only a few people have the honor of dealing with the hundreds of financially destitute students walking into the office each day. Additionally, law schools are commonly a part of a larger university and not usually a separate entity; thus, the financial aid office in the law school is often a "front" for the general financial aid office of the entire university. In turn, your financial aid officer may not have as much authority or wield as much decision-making power as you may think. Thus, save your "I'm mad as hell, and I'm not going to take this anymore" speech for the long line at the DMV, because odds are, it's not going to get you anywhere at the financial aid office.

Getting angry at the law school financial aid representative does nothing but frustrate you and the rep. Remember that handing off your forms to your law school financial aid office is only the commencement of a demonic Rube Goldberg–like trail of bureaucratic handoffs: from the law school, to the main financial aid office, to the government, back to the school, to the bank, back to the government, then to some loan shark in the Bronx who will break your kneecaps if you default, back to the government, and again to the bank where it finally ends up back at the school. The reason your forms have been delayed may be because Bill at the main campus office spilled his Triple Non-Fat No-Foam Quasi-Grande Vanilla Raspberry Nut Latte all over them, not necessarily that your financial office "forgot" (but don't necessarily rule that option out either).

Now here's what happens if you're nice to your financial aid office: It may let you know about a new kind of scholarship or low-interest loan. Or, if you're really a brown-noser, the office may send off your forms to whatever agency they need to go to right then and there, shaving a few days or even a week off the waiting time. If you're ranting and raving about how much you need your money, realize that the financial aid office gets the same whining from almost every student who walks through the door and will spend more time trying to get you to shut up and get out of the office than giving you a time- or money-saving tip. Remember, behind the forms and policies, the people at financial aid are human, too.

2. FOLLOW UP ON EVERY CONTACT WITH THE FINANCIAL AID OFFICE OR ANY AGENCY OR PERSON YOU DEAL WITH WHEN DOING ANYTHING WITH FINANCIAL AID.

This means the school, the government, the bank, or that loan shark in the Bronx who's gonna bust your kneecaps.

Good assertive follow-ups are different from ticking people off. These calls serve two very mathematical purposes: They remind "x" bureaucrat that he or she was supposed to check, process, or do thing "y" for you. The calls also can serve as a confirmation of "z" information that you gave to "x" bureaucrat.

Record all calls you make regarding financial aid. That way, if something bad happens, you can simply say, "Well, I spoke to 'x' bureaucrat regarding 'y' issue on 'w' day. I reconfirmed 'z' information of 'y' issue with 'x' bureaucrat over the phone the next day."

3. MAKE A COPY OF EVERYTHING, EVEN IF YOU ALREADY HAVE A CARBON COPY.

Nothing is more damning evidence of a red-tape slip-up than a nice photocopy of a form that supposedly wasn't turned in or was lost. Even if you get a carbon copy of a form (say, a promissory note for a loan), make a copy of the top page that goes to the lender and the school. Generally (as is the usual way in school administration), the student's needs are overlooked and you wind up with the last carbon copy, which is barely legible. (They told you to press hard when you filled out the application, but you didn't listen, did you?)

4. The Prime Directive: Never, ever, ever, ever turn in anything late.

In the world of financial aid, when you hand in something late, you are essentially saying, "Please, please, please delay my financial aid! I really don't want any money at all! Yes, I want to miss out on all the special considerations for scholarships! I don't care about eating this year!" Well, not exactly that . . . but close.

Remember the complicated chain of paper handoffs in Rule No. 1? Well, if you miss the beginning of the ride, you may just have to wait until everyone else gets a turn to ride the paper train before you get to go again. Few deadlines are as important and strict as financial aid, and if you miss one . . . well, may the force be with you, 'cause that's all you'll have going for you. And if you do turn something in late, refer again to Rule No. 1: If you miss a deadline, it's probably your fault, and there's no point in whining to the financial aid office that your tax forms were late because you (while the deadline passed) were still trying to figure out a way to save a few bucks on your taxes.

Not only should you not be late, but as soon as a form *can* be turned in, fill it out and turn it in. Consider this: You will probably have to fill out forms for the school's internal use, forms for both the government's use and the school's use, forms solely for the government's use, forms for assorted banks, and insurance forms for the prescriptions you'll need to calm you down after filling out the other forms. If you are late with a government application, for example, it is possible that the school will not allow you to fill out one of their forms until it receives confirmation of the government application. If you can't fill out the school's application, you won't be able to process the bank application. *Being late often sets off a chain of delays over which you have no control.* Not even Oppenheimer could have predicted such a devastating chain reaction. This will result in a few bad consequences. At best, you will get your money late (say, toward the middle of the semester). In worst-case scenarios, you may miss out on scholarships or low-interest loans (often first-come, first-served), or you may not get any money at all.

> *My school offers a plan where you can break down your tuition payments into installments over the school year. I have an airline-sponsored credit card that I use with the monthly plan. That way, I get one frequent-flyer mile for every dollar I spend. I pay off the bill every month when it comes with the money I have set aside for tuition so no interest accrues.*
>
> *By the end of the school year, despite the excessive cost of tuition, I get a round-trip flight on the house. You could say that, in my own way, I'm getting a free ride.*
>
> —DORON AZRIALY, BOSTON COLLEGE LAW SCHOOL

GATHER YOUR RESOURCES—YOU'RE IN FOR THE LONG HAUL

Hooray! It's time to figure out how the heck you'll be paying for an education that costs more per year than two mid-sized cars (or just one really large pony). How will you pay? After ruling out blood donations as an option (or after running out of blood to give), it's time to look at your resources.

First, check out what you have in terms of savings. You may want to apply any money you currently have toward tuition or living expenses while you're in school. Or you may want to use your savings for moving expenses, your new apartment, or replacing that futon with a real mattress (you'll thank yourself later). No matter what you decide to do with your savings, if any, you'll want to figure out the *total* cost of living and going to school.

For this task, every school has a pre-set budget for the school year. This budget includes tuition, fees, school supplies, rent, living expenses, and tequila (though financial aid offices will refer to that last item as generic "recreational expenses"). Budgets vary from school to school, depending mainly on location, cost of living, and tuition. For example, a private law school in Boston with tuition of $20,000 per year may have a total student budget of $38,000, while a private law school in Spokane with tuition of $20,000 per year may have a total student budget of $30,000. This is because the cost of living in Boston is much higher than in Spokane.

No matter what the budget is, think of it as a financial ceiling. If your school has set the budget to $38,000 for the school year, then the total amount of financial aid you may receive is limited to that amount. This includes grants, scholarships, and loans. All financial aid you receive is checked through your financial aid office. So if you've already borrowed $38,000 for the school year and want to borrow $5,000 to go on that steamy singles cruise in the Mediterranean, your financial aid office will politely inform the bank that you've already borrowed as much as allowed under your financial aid plan for the year. Your financial aid office will then politely inform you that you need to find a less expensive way to get a date.

So you've checked your savings. Have you begged your family for money? Don't laugh. Parents who were reluctant to pay for your four-year, nonstop decadence binge called college might be willing to help you a little bit with a serious endeavor like law school (little do they know the truth). On the flip side, parents who *did* foot the bill for your four-year, nonstop decadence binge may see that, instead of waking up safely from your undergrad stupor in a gutter, you woke up and found yourself in law school. Aghast, they may simply cut you off and never speak to you again for your desire to be a lawyer—but that's your personal issue, isn't it?

In any case, you may just want to stifle your pride and see if any close relatives might be willing to contribute to your cause.

If you have enough money to pay for the whole thing and don't ever plan on entering the financial aid office, except perhaps to ask to use the stapler, skip this chapter.

You have a little money or no money? No problem. That's where the magical world of financial aid comes in. Read on, future debtor!

The Paper Chase: Two Forms You Gotta Do

THE SCHOOL'S FINANCIAL AID APPLICATION

Remember that thing that you sent in with each application for every school you applied to? Did you make a copy? If not, please see Rule No. 3 above and give yourself a retroactive slap on the wrist. The first-year application for financial aid is usually sent in with (or shortly after) the application for admission. If not, you will receive the financial aid application if you are accepted.

Really, we don't need to tell you what to do here. As long as you follow the instructions on the form, you'll be fine. Make sure, though, to send in all requested attachments. Schools will often ask for a copy of your income tax return. If you fail to send in the return, look forward to a financial aid delay. Remember that financial aid stuff is generally not processed until *all* components are present. In this case, your application would be collecting dust on a shelf until you sent in your tax form. Don't forget that these applications can take up to two months to process (although they average a few weeks), so if you decide to wait until the last minute, you've guaranteed yourself delayed financial aid.

THE FREE APPLICATION FOR FEDERAL STUDENT AID

Whoo-hoo! It's free! Calm down, Sparky—just the application is free, not the money. The FAFSA (yes, more acronyms brought to you by The Government Who Invented Acronyms, or TGWIA) is a 100-percent free application. It also happens to be the birth mother of your financial aid. A great deal of data is collected from this form and run through a government computer, which allows Big Brother to know that much more about you. Feel comfy now? Good, let's proceed.

With your No. 2 pencil, follow the instructions step by step. (Do *not* use a No. 3 pencil, as this will cause a chemical reaction with the special government ink and cause the FAFSA to self-combust. Actually, nothing exciting will happen, but wouldn't that be cool?) It's a pretty straightforward application, but just in case you can't figure out what to do, the federal government has provided useful instructions like this one for the driver's license number section: "Write in your current driver's license number and the abbreviation of the state in which the license was issued . . . " Whew! Good thing Uncle Sam was there to hold my hand through that toughie.

Despite the obviousness of some of the sections, though, you will want to read the instructions because other sections have specific requirements, while still others refer you to a worksheet in the back of the booklet. Also, don't forget to read the section on how to get the FAFSA results sent to the schools of your choice. Make sure that you have the proper school code to fill in on the FAFSA; otherwise, the school will not receive the report and your aid will be (you guessed it) delayed.

First important point about the FAFSA: The instructions make it clear what you, graduate student, either dependent or independent, are to fill out. By law, you are not required to fill in parental information on the FAFSA in order to receive federal aid. *However, your school may require you to fill out the FAFSA parental information section to qualify for school-based aid. Make sure you check with the financial aid office on this!* This mistake has cost many students time and benefits in the financial aid process.

"That's not fair! I don't want to bug my parents for their income and tax information. I'm an adult." News flash: Get over yourself. The school will do whatever it can to make it seem as if you don't need aid. This strategy often includes basing your financial need on your parents' income, even if you don't rely on them for support or haven't spoken to them in years. If your parents can claim you as a dependent on their taxes, even if they don't actually claim you, your school is allowed to figure that into the formula to determine the extent of your financial need.

Don't lie on your forms. People will tell you to "make yourself look as poor as possible." Schools generally have a set formula on how to distribute their financial aid and are pretty good at catching low-income fabrications. Realize that, if you get caught, you may face serious consequences, such as denial of aid or administrative discipline. And, besides, lying is very unattractive.

Along with the no-lying thing is a much more benign, obvious point: Be consistent. Your numbers on the FAFSA should match your numbers on the school application, as they should match the numbers on any loan application. Separately, it doesn't make a difference, but if your financial aid office gets ahold of your FAFSA and sees that you have even the slightest discrepancy of information (especially regarding income), the financial aid office will likely put a hold on your application until the discrepancy is resolved. If this hold means waiting a few weeks for you to produce documents showing the correct information, so be it. *Always make sure that you use the correct information to avoid delays—and to avoid looking like a moron.* It's not as bad as lying: people will still love you, but they'll pity you for your ineptitude.

Once you send in your FAFSA, you can relax for a couple of weeks. But that's not the last you've seen of your FAFSA. Like a lost puppy, the FAFSA will come wandering back to you in about a month, but this time it's changed its name. You are now looking at the lean and mean SAR (Student Aid Report). This form is basically the aid office's "rough draft" of your application. You just need to run through it, correct any mistakes, sign it, and send it back. Check again that you put the proper school codes on it (call your school to confirm if you're not absolutely sure—sometimes law schools have different codes from their undergraduate university counterparts). Once you send that SAR back to the dark annals of the Federal Student Aid Processing Center (FSAPC), it'll send a final copy in a few weeks to you and your school.

You may obtain an electronic version of the FAFSA on the World Wide Web at the Department of Education's Web site. This downloadable software gives you step-by-step instructions as you fill out the form and then transmits the data using your modem. The information is *instantly* processed, and your SAR is done within a week. Now that's service! However, if you are concerned with Internet security, be aware that you will be sending personal information over the Internet.

THE LETTER THAT SEALS YOUR FATE

If all of this sounds complicated, it's not. Just remember the four simple rules and you'll be fine. If you've done everything correctly, you will receive an award letter from the financial aid office. Unlike Ed McMahon's award letters, yours will not say, "YOU COULD ALREADY BE A BILLIONAIRE!" in big gaudy letters on the envelope. Oh no. Your award letter from financial aid is nothing but a paradox. Students are excited to get their "award" letters, but then they open them and are disappointed to read the following: "Congratulations! You, student, have jumped through the red tape hoops of both the federal government *and* a university's financial aid system. We have reviewed your application and your reward is as follows: $8,500 subsidized Stafford loans; $10,000 unsubsidized Stafford loans. You may now apply for loans. Good luck, bucko." What the hell kind of award is that? That's right, friend, you've essentially been awarded the opportunity to go into debt.

The award letter is the school's way of distributing available in-school resources. If you're not happy with the results, there's always the appeal process. Say you really think you deserve one of those super-duper low-interest school-granted loans. Your appeal letter would simply state that you feel your award was a little on the skimpy side and that your financial circumstances merit a review. Often, your award will be minimal if you have worked for at least one year before you entered school (as the school may be calculating your need off of your income tax return from last year, when you were pulling down oodles of cash that you didn't bother saving) or if you can still be claimed as a dependent on your parents' taxes (as the school may be basing your need off your parents' income tax return). Either way, this may have a serious effect on need-based aid.

THE TWO GENERAL FORMS OF FINANCIAL AID: SCHOLARSHIPS AND LOANS

SCHOOL HANDOUTS

At the beginning of the year, your school has certain scholarships set aside. Perhaps these scholarships are need-based or are based on your undergraduate grades. Whatever the reason they are given, there are only a limited number available. Realize that if you don't get awarded one of these scholarships, fellowships, or grants, an appeal might be tough because the school has already awarded all of the scholarships for the school year. Also, it is not uncommon for these scholarships to be automatically renewed by the school for the student every year. Hence, if there are a limited number of these scholarships, and they carry on with the same student each year, odds are that most of these scholarships won't be redistributed.

That is why it is crucial, especially the first year, to get in all financial aid forms on time. If your financial aid is delayed, you may very well miss out on the distribution period, and if that happens, there's a good chance that you've locked yourself out for the next two years, as well. Ouch. Breaking Rule No. 4 hurts, doesn't it?

OUTSIDE SCHOLARSHIPS

These are up to you. There are numerous scholarships out there for law students, whether the scholarships are law-related or not. The problem with outside scholarships is that nobody is going to hold your hand and help you find them. Possibly the best resource would be the financial aid office at your school. There are usually a couple of gigantic scholarship list books in the office that you can flip through. Each listing gives a brief description of the scholarship and whom to write to for more information. Your financial aid office may also have a list of outside scholarships commonly attained by students at your school.

Scholarships come in all shapes and sizes. You may qualify for a scholarship because your father was a tuna fisherman; you may qualify because your hometown has a little-known fund to help homegrown kids go to graduate school; you may qualify because your hair is blue and you like to dance naked in the snow. The point is that there are thousands of scholarships out there with thousands of different qualifications, and there's no telling which ones you qualify for unless you get down and research.

Don't get all excited, though. The bulk of scholarships range from a couple hundred dollars to a couple thousand. While free money is always nice, a couple hundred dollars hardly makes a dent in today's law school education market. Make sure you check every possibility to uncover the greatest number of leads. Religion, gender, ethnicity, college major, nationality, community service, and prior academic performance are all possible factors in determining the qualifications of scholarship applicants.

If you do receive an outside grant, scholarship, or fellowship, you will have to inform your financial aid office so they can factor that little prize into your financial aid portfolio and readjust your award. Remember the ceiling of the annual student budget? It applies to scholarships, too. This is so you don't run out and buy a car with your new money. But wouldn't that be nice?

LOANS: THE DARK MISTRESS OF EDUCATIONAL FINANCING

If you couldn't score any scholarships or grants, don't worry; a good portion of students rely solely on loans for their financial aid package. The question is what kind of loans do you use?

First in line are need-based loans. These are either sponsored by the school or they come in the form of a Federal Perkins Loan (FPL). Again, there are a limited number of these loans to give out, so if you do want to qualify as need-based, you *must* apply on time. Generally, need-based loans have a fixed low-interest rate of around 5 percent and are capped off somewhere around $5,000 a year. Check with your financial aid office to see what need-based loans are available and if there are any published criteria of qualification for these need-based loans.

THE STAFFORD LOAN: YOUR FRIEND

Possibly the greatest source of financial aid is Stafford loans. If you're asking, "Man, does it take an act of Congress to get financial aid around here?" the answer is yes. Stafford loans are kissed with presidential and congressional seals of approval. Relatively low-interest loans for students that are guaranteed by the government, Staffords are around to make educational financing a little easier and a bit less expensive. At the very minimum, your award letter will probably include Stafford loans.

There are two types of Stafford loans: subsidized and unsubsidized. As a law student, you may borrow up to $8,500 per year in subsidized Stafford loans. A subsidized loan in this case means that the government will pay the interest while you are enrolled in school. Unsubsidized Stafford loans have an annual cap of $10,000. These loans are still low interest, but the government does not pay for the interest that accrues while you are enrolled in school. You didn't think that Congress would be *that* generous, did you?

You can get these loans from any lender that participates in the Stafford loan program. Look for nonprofit lending agencies, such as the Access Group, that specialize in low-interest Stafford loans. In addition, because the government guarantees these loans, you don't need to worry so much about shaky or bad credit. Unless you have some hideous financial skeleton in the closet, approval for these loans is rarely a problem.

Depending on the lender you choose, there are a variety of repayment plans. Usually, repayment starts anywhere from six to nine months after you have ceased full-time enrollment at school. Repayment terms vary from 10 years to 15 years to 20 years. Keep in mind that with a shorter plan, like 10 years, you will pay less over the long run than you would by paying over 15 years, despite the fact that on the 10-year plan, monthly payments will be higher than with a longer plan. The longer plans cost more overall because, while monthly payments for a 15- or 20-year plan will be lower, interest will accrue over a substantially longer period of time. Having a higher overall payment is not necessarily bad, however, especially if you need the extra cash on a monthly basis or think you can earn a decent return on that extra monthly cash. When the time comes after graduation, you can discuss repayment terms with your lender. Most lenders are flexible in suiting payment options to your needs. After all, they don't want a student debtor to fall behind in payments just because the monthly rate was too high.

Okay, so we've got over 18 grand tucked away. Hey! That doesn't even cover tuition! What gives? That's right, Stafford caps haven't been raised recently and thus have not kept up with the annual tuition hikes at most schools. So where do you turn? Before you take the last step to covering your financial needs, make sure you have checked all other sources: family, personal savings, scholarships, and so on. You'll want to check these last sources one more time because the final step is a painful one.

THE PRIVATE LOAN

When applying for private loans, you need two things: good credit and a strong stomach. Good credit to get approved for the loan. A strong stomach to stomach the high-interest rate. Now is a good time to discuss your credit history. If you haven't already ordered a credit report from Experian (formerly TRW), Trans Union, or Equifax, the three major credit-reporting services, you should do so immediately. Remember that final cable bill you never paid your freshman year in college when you moved for the summer? It's on the report. You've been consistently paying off your credit cards late? It's noted on the report. *Don't underestimate the power of credit reports.* Lenders will be looking at the very same report. A single unpaid cable bill or consistently late credit card payments are enough to deny approval for a loan. And if you ask any person who's been rejected for a private loan, it's a bad, bad, bad feeling.

Most lenders will tell you exactly what their limits are on credit glitches, so you can check beforehand to see whether you can be approved. Some of the nonprofit lenders, such as Nellie Mae or Access, don't require you to have a co-signer for a private loan, but most do. The co-signer is usually your parent or another "adult" figure in your life. The co-signer for your loan acts as a backup in the event that you default on your loan or fall behind in payments. Your co-signer is just as responsible as you are for the payment of the loan when it comes to liability.

Check with your financial aid office to see whether there are any state-localized loan programs. Some states have a private loan program designed specifically for schools in their state. The Massachusetts Educational Funding Authority, for example, offers low-interest fixed-rate loans to students who are attending colleges in Massachusetts. Credit is still important, but the interest rate with these types of private loans is significantly lower than it would be with private banks.

Private loans are a *huge* financial responsibility, and you should consider whether you are willing to take on that burden. How much will you be borrowing over your entire three years? How much do you realistically plan on earning when you graduate? These are a couple of the many questions you need to consider when you are looking at the possibility of private loans.

A final word on private loans: If you are going to seek out a private loan, try to have a backup plan. Not infrequently, students apply for a private loan and fail to get approval for that loan in the middle of the semester. How will the student pay for the remainder of tuition and living expenses? If you are going the private loan route, try to get it done as early as possible, so you are sure that you actually do have the loan by the beginning of the semester.

OTHER HELPFUL FINANCIAL FACTS

WORKING DURING THE SCHOOL YEAR

Law schools generally frown upon students working during their first year. Some schools actually forbid students to work as One-Ls. When necessity strikes, however, and you need money to survive, work becomes a practical option. Whether it's waiting tables or working as a security guard, there are many ways to pay the bills. A legal job is not a must and might be hard to attain as a first-year student. Many students actually prefer to hold a non-legal job during the school year simply to avoid having to think about law for a few hours a week. (See Chapter 9, "Working During Law School," for more detailed information.)

Alternatively, you may try to apply for work-study at school. Work-study is a form of financial aid and is deducted from your annual student budget. Usually work-study positions are on campus, ranging from a professor's research assistant to a computer lab monitor. During the school year, many students like to do work-study in rather sedentary jobs where they can study while they "work," such as the computer monitor position mentioned above. While work-study positions don't pay much, they have some great advantages: They either give you the chance to research for a professor in a field you are interested in or allow you to sit on your rump and study for classes that you aren't really interested in, but are getting called on the next day, so you *have* to study. In addition, because work-study is usually on campus, you won't have the hassle of running to the other side of town after school for your job. Check with your financial aid office on how to apply for work-study and what the qualifications are. (See Chapter 9, "Working During Law School," for more information on work-study programs.)

LOAN FORGIVENESS: CAN YOU SPARE A MONTHLY PAYMENT?

Some schools have a loan forgiveness program. If a student chooses to work in a public interest field and earns a substantially lower income than his or her private law firm counterparts, a school with a loan forgiveness program may partially or wholly subsidize the student's loan payments. Requirements, application procedures, and programs vary widely, so check with your financial aid office about your school's loan forgiveness policies.

LOAN CONSOLIDATION: GIVE ME ONE HUGE LUMP SUM, PLEASE!

Picture this: You've taken out the max in Staffords every year for three years. That's six loans. That's a lot of debt to keep track of and monitor. Enter the federal government. It's possible to consolidate all your federal loans (including previous undergrad loans) into one big loan. The advantage to consolidation is that once your federal loans are consolidated, you only have to make one payment per month to cover all your federal loans. This consolidation may allow you to have greater control over your finances when you begin working and are struggling to make sense of the barrage of loan repayments that will begin precisely six to nine months after graduation. By consolidating, you also may be able to extend your loan repayment schedule and make lower or higher monthly interest payments (which may be good or bad). This is not Monopoly® money, so you may want to consult an expert, such as your financial aid officer, to see whether consolidation makes sense in your particular situation. Unfortunately, consolidation applies only to federal loans, not private loans, unless you have private loans from the same lender and that lender has a consolidation program for its loans.

DEBT UPON DEBT UPON DEBT: UNDERGRADUATE LOANS

Already have prior loans from college? No worries. The rumor is that some students actually decide to go to law school simply to avoid paying their undergraduate loans for a few more years. Once you are enrolled at your law school, you can usually get payments for your undergraduate loans deferred until after law school graduation. This feature also permits you to consolidate your graduate federal loans with your undergraduate loans.

As for a total cap on Stafford loans, you may not exceed $138,500. This means that your federal loans for education prior to law school may not exceed $83,000. If your loans are up to this level, odds are that you have been attending collegiate-level schools for quite some time, have more degrees than a Kelvin thermometer, and are getting a J.D. "just for kicks."

For more information, your financial aid office can direct you to the proper forms and procedure to defer your previous loans. Keep in mind, however, that you will have to pay back your student loans one day when you run out of graduate programs to attend.

DECLARING BANKRUPTCY TO GET RID OF YOUR LOANS

Dream on. They have laws against that, you know (as thousands of disappointed students discover on the first day of Bankruptcy class each year). Shame on you, naughty, naughty debtor.

GETTING YOUR MONEY

Suppose you've done everything right: You turned in all your forms on time, you made copies of everything, you followed up on all of your calls, and you managed not to irritate too many financial aid people. Well, here comes the money! Because everything is routed through financial aid, scholarships and loan checks are routed from that office to student accounts. You will be called in for the ritualistic endorsement of your check, which is the closest you'll ever get to it, because immediately after endorsement, the student loan officer will snatch the check out of your hands and drop it directly into the school's bank account.

Any money you get through financial aid is usually first applied directly toward your tuition (those schools know something or another about being smart). After your entire tuition bill has been satisfied, you will receive a refund check for the surplus amount. Depending on how you chose to do your financial aid, this check will cover or supplement your living expenses for the year. *Remember, though, that you might need to use some of this money next semester to cover tuition that is not automatically covered by scholarship or Stafford credits on your account (tuition is usually charged per semester, instead of in one lump sum).*

LIVING LIKE A STUDENT

Welcome to the world of the poor, the wretched, the law student. If you've been holding down a job for the past couple of years, making a nice plump living, kiss that lifestyle good-bye for a couple of years. You are now on a much smaller budget. Remember Ramen soup? Reacquaint yourself with that old friend.

It's actually not that bad, but remember that you won't have a paycheck coming in every couple of weeks, so for all practical purposes, assume that what you have in the bank is all that you have to your name. Invest in a financial program for your computer, such as Microsoft Money™ or Intuit's Quicken™. These applications not only help you balance your checkbook, but also keep track of what and where you spend your money. If at the end of the month you check out what you've spent your money on and are treated to a pie chart that is three-quarters red and the legend says that "red" equals "beer fund," you may need to rethink your spending habits.

Your financial aid has been calculated to last for a single school year. This is usually about nine to 10 months. Don't count on using that money for the summer. You don't want to stretch yourself too thin. In fact, try to under-budget yourself each month and put a little money aside for a nice trip somewhere on spring break (especially if you go to school in the Northeast, where spring break normally lands somewhere in, oh, winter).

ONE LAST POINT

So you've made it through the jungle of forms, red tape, endless phone holds, ambiguous answers, and unfathomable fear of not being able to find a job to pay off all of this debt.

Here's what you do next: Forget about it all! The moment you've deposited or signed your last check is the moment you need to accept the fact that you are in school to learn, not to worry about money. So you'll be in debt—most law students are. Under no circumstances should you let your fear of not being able to repay loans influence your first-year experience. As long as you stay realistic about your financial aid and your career expectations, you'll stay sane and happy (which, as you'll find, have become variable terms in the world of law school).

—by Dan Ralls

CHAPTER 9

Working During Law School

TO WORK OR NOT TO WORK

Working during law school can be very rewarding if you find the right job, with the right hours and the right pay. It can help round out your law school education and give you the practical real-world experience that your classes can't give you. It can also help ease the financial strain that most law students feel. Perhaps most importantly, a job during law school can give you a good perspective on what it's like to be a lawyer and show you that "yes, there is life outside of law school." The decision of whether to get a job during the school year is not an easy one, however, and you should fully consider your options before you decide to embark on the job search.

QUESTIONS TO ASK BEFORE STARTING YOUR JOB SEARCH

1. WHY SHOULD YOU GET A JOB?

There are several great reasons to work during the school year. First, a job during the school year can help ease the burden of those heavy loans that most law students carry. Second, a job can round out the law school experience by balancing what at times can seem like a very abstract academic schedule with real-world, tangible experiences. Third, a job during the school year can give you an arena to practice and hone weekly the skills and tools that you are learning in your classes. Finally, for students who start law school directly out of college, a job during the school year may be necessary to keep you from getting "burned out" from many years of nothing but schooling!

On the other hand, you should think very carefully before you decide to take on a job during the school year, *especially during the first year*. During the first year of law school, students have little time to do anything but study. Many law schools even have restrictions against first-year students working during the school year. Furthermore, most law students intern or clerk during their summers and thus working during the school year is not the only way to get good legal experience. Finally, most law schools offer a wide variety of extracurricular activities, such as writing on a law journal, getting involved in a special interest group, or participating in the law school student government. Working during the school year may prevent you from taking full advantage of those activities.

2. WHAT TYPE OF JOB SHOULD YOU GET?

The first thing you should decide is whether you want a legal or non-legal job. If your motivations for getting a job are purely financial, a non-legal job may be a welcome alternative to "legalese" and the Socratic Method. Furthermore, this may be your last chance to be a house painter or a bartender. Finally, non-legal jobs are often less stressful than legal ones. Not all legal jobs are stressful, however, and as long as you are working, you may want to do something that "boosts your resume."

> *I have chosen to work in a non-legal position because it is non-legal. Despite my love for the law, it is a relief to know that I have a couple of hours each week during which I do not have to think about*

law and during which I stop analyzing everything I hear, read, and write. This year, I decided to waitress at a country club in my hometown, and, although waiting tables can be stressful at times, it is a different kind of stress. It is busy work that amazingly prevents my mind from wandering to legal issues. Well, sometimes I think of potential slips and falls, but mostly I simply welcome the opportunity to get away from studying law, reading law, writing law, and breathing law. Furthermore, working in a non-legal position provides me with the opportunity to associate with people who do not have law constantly on their minds. If you are thinking about working during the academic semester, consider a non-legal job. Waiting tables, for example, is flexible and easy, and the pay is pretty good. If you are afraid that choosing such a job will prevent you from gaining legal experience, do not be concerned. There is plenty of time during the summers to gain that experience. The most important thing is that the job you do choose, legal or non-legal, should be fun and, above all, should not detract from your studies.

—JULIE CURRAN, BOSTON COLLEGE LAW SCHOOL

If you decide to pursue a legal job, there are several types: volunteer, research, and paid. The different types suit different interests and needs; thus, it may be useful for you to determine exactly why you are getting a job before you decide which type to pursue.

Volunteer work, though non-paying, can be very sophisticated. Chances are, you do not have much experience in the legal field. Volunteering is a great way to get good experience. After all, most people will not turn down free work. Volunteering can also be fulfilling because you may be working for public interest groups or indigent clients. Finally, volunteering can occasionally lead to a paid job, either after law school or further along in your law school career.

A research position is also a great job because, while it is still very academic, you will be rewarded for your labors beyond a mere grade on your report card. Research jobs can be either paid or for-credit. In addition, if your research ultimately leads to a publication, you will usually be credited for your work. Most research jobs are for professors at your law school, but there may also be research jobs available with lawyers and law firms associated with your law school. Some research positions may even be non-law related. One thing you will become an expert at by the end of law school is research, and others will want to take advantage of that expertise.

Paid jobs are usually the most sought after for obvious reasons, and therefore the most difficult to procure. They can range from clerking at a law firm or government office to working at your law school's cafeteria. Some types of paid work are obviously more demanding than others, and the level of commitment required usually correlates with the amount you are paid.

> **TIP:** Most law schools offer an abundance of legal jobs, especially for second- and third-year students. If you want a legal job, seek one out through one of the resources listed below. While paid legal jobs are a little more difficult to find, they are still fairly abundant, if you are not too picky.

3. WHAT ARE SOME JOBS YOU CAN GET?

The range of jobs that are available to law students is endless. You have a college degree, and for many of you, law school is a second career. Thus, you are qualified to do a lot more than when you were in college. There is nothing to stop you from taking a professional job outside the law profession. The problem with such a commitment is that someone who has not been through law school may not understand how demanding law school is and may require more of your time than you can give.

Probably the easiest types of jobs to handle are on-campus jobs, such as working in your cafeteria or library. These jobs often do not pay much, but they offer flexible hours that are usually very compatible with your school schedule. Examples of on-campus or school-related jobs include:

Food Service Jobs: Duties include serving meals, preparing food, and performing custodial work.

School Library Positions: This may entail working at the reference desk, shelving books, or even doing research for university faculty.

Tutoring Positions: This may involve tutoring other law students or, if your school has an undergraduate program, tutoring undergraduate students.

Residence Hall Positions: Most schools need residential advisors for both their undergraduate dorms and their graduate housing. The best part about this job is that it often includes free room and board.

Clerical Work: Many departments need students who have office skills, such as typing.

Bookstore Jobs: Employment in your law school bookstore may be a good way to get a discount on those oh-so-expensive law books.

Administrative Work: Often the dean's office or other administrative offices may need help managing their administrative duties. Work may include inputting information in computer systems, organizing files, and keeping track of records.

Teaching Assistant Positions: This may involve working with a first-year writing class or other similar class. Your university may also allow you to apply for a teaching assistantship at the undergraduate school.

4. How much time will the job take?

Consider your potential time commitment before taking a job. Beware of "snowball" jobs—jobs that start out manageable and then grow and grow until you are overwhelmed. A good way to avoid this type of avalanche is to make clear to your employer from the outset that you are a law student with limited availability and a demanding school schedule. Instead of saying, "I can work about 10 to 15 hours per week," say, "I am only available on Mondays and Wednesdays between noon and 5 P.M." You should also plan ahead of time for exams and holidays, making sure your employer knows from the outset that you will need flexibility around midterms and finals, or around whatever other school-related crises may occur.

Another thing you should consider is how much commuting time will be involved in actually getting to your job. You may only be working 10 hours a week, but if it takes you an hour to get to work and an hour to get home every time, your hours away from home quickly add up.

Also, don't forget sanity time! If you are working all day and going to classes at night, you might soon realize that you have no time to do anything in between but eat and sleep. And when did you plan to read those 100 pages for Civil Procedure?

The number of hours you can realistically work each week will depend largely on your schedule. During the first year, you will be lucky if you can squeeze in five hours per week for any non-law school activity. In the third year, you may find that you can easily work 20-plus hours per week. Before you agree to work a set number of hours, you should sit down and figure out exactly how many hours a week you will need for classes, studying, and free time. Then plan your work schedule accordingly. You may find it helpful to go to two or three weeks of classes before you start work so that you fall into a comfortable schedule.

WHERE DO YOU LOOK AND WHOM DO YOU ASK?

I have had great luck finding jobs while attending law school. In the spring of my first year, when I found myself with a little more time on my hands, I decided to get a part-time legal job. I had started law school straight out of college and therefore did not have a lot of experience under my belt. At that point, although I needed money, my priority was just to get some legal experience. I went to the Pro Bono Students of America office and expressed my interest in environmental law. Within about a week, I had procured a non-paying internship at a government agency right down the street from my law school. I worked there pro bono all spring, and then they offered me a paid position for the summer. I am a third-year student now and I still work there part-time during the school year as a paid law clerk.

During my second year, I was in the financial aid office one day when one of my first-year professors walked into the office. When he saw me, he asked me if I was a work-study recipient, and I said yes (at my law school, only work-study students can be research assistants). He said, "Great! I need a new research assistant and you're just the one for the job!" I was feeling especially crunched financially that semester, and the extra money from being a research assistant really helped out. You never know when a job is going to pop up and bite you on the nose, so keep a lookout!

—JOANNA L. GIORGIO, BOSTON COLLEGE LAW SCHOOL

Remember that you don't know when a job is going to pop up, so make sure you explore every possibility. Any situation can be a networking opportunity, so get used to taking advantage of those opportunities when they present themselves.

PROFESSORS

One of your greatest resources for finding a job is your professors, especially your first-year professors, who tend to know you particularly well. Don't be afraid to approach your professors for work. Most professors hire one to two research assistants per semester, sometimes more. If a professor likes and respects you from having you in her class, she will surely be happy to hire you as a research assistant. Moreover, many professors do consulting work for outside law firms or organizations. They may need students to help them in this research as well. Even if your favorite professor is not hiring any research assistants at the moment, she will probably be happy to recommend you to a colleague who does need an assistant. Remember that your professors also have many connections to the "outside world" and thus may be able to help you get your foot in the door at a law firm, government agency, or judge's chambers. Professors are a great networking resource, and helping you get a job is ultimately one of the things they are paid for—don't be afraid to ask them for help!

> **TIP:** Another great reason to work for a professor is that working together provides a perfect way to get to know your professor well enough so that he or she is willing to go to bat for you should you need a recommendation for a judicial clerkship or other legal position.

CAREER SERVICES

While at most law schools the career services office is geared toward helping students find summer or permanent placements, it is still a

WORKING DURING LAW SCHOOL **149**

great resource for finding work during the school year. Your career services office may have postings of job opportunities within your community. It also may have information on law firms or organizations who have hired students in the past. Even if these employers are not presently hiring, sending them a copy of your resume can't hurt and often leads to a job a few months down the road. Finally, your career services office is generally helpful in providing you with a good strategy to find a job that is perfect for you. The career counselors most likely know about all the different types of legal jobs and the pros and cons of each type. You may want to sit down with a counselor before you start your job search to discuss the possibilities.

PRO BONO STUDENTS OF AMERICA

Pro Bono Students of America (PBSA) is an organization that acts as a liaison between your law school and your legal community. It is designed to connect students who want to work during the school year with public-sector employers who are looking for legal help. Your PBSA office will have access to a database with a wide variety of opportunities that match your interests, whether you are interested in animal rights or health care law or something else entirely. You can also access PBSA directly through the Internet. The only potential drawback is that "pro bono" means "for good" or, in lay terms, "for free." A few of the jobs are paid, but most are not.

> **TIP:** Most law schools have an internal public interest organization, similar to the National Association of Public Interest Law (NAPIL), which may provide funding for students who work in the public sector. Thus, even if your pro bono job is a non-paying job, you may still be able to get a stipend through your school's public interest organization. Additionally, if your pro bono job is a qualifying work-study job, and you are a work-study recipient, you can fund your job that way.

FINANCIAL AID DEPARTMENT

If you are a work-study recipient, you should have no problem finding a job. Your financial aid department should have a listing of all legal and non-legal jobs available for work-study recipients. In fact, many of the on-campus jobs are available only to work-study students.

Applying For the Job

If you are interested in an on-campus job, typically the application process is simple: You check the job postings, find one you are interested in, make a phone call, and start working. The application process for a research or administrative assistant will involve a bit more screening. The professor or faculty member who needs an assistant will want to find someone whom the professor feels is compatible, smart, and responsible, so the professor may even conduct interviews. The process, however, will usually be pretty informal.

Most other types of legal jobs will probably require sending the prospective employer a resume and cover letter. Based on your resume and cover letter, the prospective employer will decide whether he or she wants to interview you. Basically, the employer will want to see whether, on paper, you are qualified for the job. Some of the qualifications will be tangible—experience, education, grades, and skills; other qualifications will be intangible—personality, character, interests, and attitude. Therefore, it is important to be able to convey all of this information in your resume and cover letter. You can't get the job if you can't even get in front of the employer for an interview!

Once you are selected for an interview, the process can vary depending on the formality of the job for which you are applying. In some cases, the prospective employer will simply want to talk to you on the phone, tell you a little bit about the job, learn a little bit about you, and then hire you on the spot. In other cases, the process will entail a screening interview and then a "callback" interview. As a rule, however, the application process for jobs during the school year is not as rigorous as the process for summer jobs, which you'll find out about in the next chapter.

GENERAL APPLICATION PROCESS

1. WRITE YOUR COVER LETTER.

Your cover letter should be tailored to the job you are applying for—*do not send a "form" cover letter!* The general purpose of the cover letter is to convey information to the prospective employer that is not apparent from your resume. Your career services office should have sample cover letters that you can look at to get a sense of the general format. The most important thing to remember is that you want the reader of your cover letter to come away with a sense of who you are, why you want this job, and what you have to offer. Depending on the job you are applying for, your prospective employer may have stacks and stacks of resumes to review. Your cover letter may be your only chance to distinguish yourself, so use it!

2. WRITE YOUR RESUME.

Again, your career services office should have copies of sample formats for resumes. Your resume should be neat, organized, concise (limit it to *one* page), and grammatically *perfect*. There are no excuses for grammatical errors or misspelled words on a resume. Have a law school friend or someone from your career services office review your resume before you send it out.

Don't hesitate to toot your own horn on your resume—think of it as your one and only opportunity to brag about all of your accomplishments without feeling pompous!

3. INTERVIEW FOR THE JOB.

The most important advice about interviewing is this: *Be yourself!* Of course, you want to highlight your strengths and minimize your weaknesses, but you can do that without pretending to be someone that you are not. An interview can be stressful enough without feeling like you have to convince your interviewer that you know everything there is to know about computers when you don't even know how to turn one on! Also, don't be defensive about your apparent weaknesses. Be confident and secure, and answer every question truthfully and honestly (in the best light possible, of course). Chapter 11, "Interviewing," will provide you with much more detailed information about how to interview successfully.

So, there it is, everything you need to know about working during the school year in a nutshell! As mentioned earlier, working during law school is not for everyone. If you carefully prioritize your responsibilities, needs, and interests before you embark on the job search, however, working during law school can be one of the most rewarding and educational experiences that you have during your entire law school career.

—by Joanna L. Giorgio

CHAPTER 10

The Summer Job Search

The first day of my first-year summer job was the worst day of my life. I was very nervous when I arrived at work because I knew they were expecting me to do all kinds of things, and I felt like I had no idea what to do—like my first year of law school had left me very ill-prepared. So I stumbled around the office for a day or so, but then I realized a couple of important things. First, I realized that I had actually learned something during my first year of law school—or, at least, I had been given the tools of legal research so I could go out and find whatever it was that I needed. Second, I realized that everyone else was in the same position that I was, no matter where they had gone to law school— you just cannot be expected to know everything there is to know on the first day. As these two things began to sink into my head, I relaxed and began to enjoy my job and to take advantage of the incredible learning experience it presented to me.

—THOMAS SHARP, YALE LAW SCHOOL

GIVE YOURSELF SOME BREATHING ROOM

First semester, first year of law school can be quite an overwhelming experience: more reading than you know what to do with, memos, briefs, the Socratic Method, and on and on. Add to that a summer job search and you could have a recipe for disaster. Fortunately, one of the first things your law school's career development office will tell you is that, under the American Bar Association guidelines, contact with potential employers should not begin until late in the first semester (after December 1). Take this guideline seriously. The late starting date should come as a relief to you and should take some pressure off at the beginning of an otherwise stressful time. Early in the semester, put the job search in the back of your mind. Get acclimated to law school life and focus primarily on your classes and assignments. Use your energy to prepare each night for the next day's classes, to get involved in law school organizations, and to develop friendships with other classmates. Maybe even treat yourself to a beer night or a movie once in a while.

With this caveat in mind, the rest of this chapter attempts to give you an overview of job possibilities for your first-year summer and some practical tips for approaching the job search as a first-year law student. At the end of the chapter, there will be a brief description of the second-year summer job search. As this is a book designed primarily for first-years, you will not be burdened with too much information about your job search in the years ahead.

BROAD GUIDELINES FOR YOUR FIRST-YEAR SUMMER JOB SEARCH

While there is little you can or should do in the way of contacting employers during the first few months of law school, there are some things you can do throughout the first semester to make your life easier when that day comes.

1. Narrow your focus.

Confine the extent of your search during the first few months to narrowing your focus as to what types of jobs you want to pursue and where you want to pursue them. Ask yourself what you want to get out of the summer. Set some goals.

The possibilities are truly endless. Think about whether you will be applying for public interest jobs, firm jobs, legislative/policy jobs, a clerkship, a study program, or whether you will be pursuing some other type of opportunity, either legal or non-legal in nature.

Take some time to think about your particular interests in the law, those you came to law school hoping to pursue and those you may have developed in law school. Keep these interests in mind as you begin to narrow your focus.

2. Watch out for deadlines.

Remember that the application process will differ depending on which avenue you pursue—deadlines and procedures for applying may vary depending on the type of job and organization. Be aware of job-specific deadlines and application procedures.

3. Consider splitting your summer between two jobs.

If you have several interests, think about splitting your summer. Many first-years do so, spending the first half at one organization and the second half somewhere else. It's a great way to double your experience, though there are some drawbacks, too (you may not get a full experience; your experience may be rushed).

4. Try out a new city.

As part of focusing your search, use the first few months of law school to decide where you would like to work. Many students look upon their first summer job as a way to explore not only a new legal opportunity, but also a new city or even a new country.

5. SEEK ADVICE FROM SECOND- AND THIRD-YEAR STUDENTS.

Second- and third-year students at your law school are excellent resources. As you attempt to narrow your focus, ask them questions about their summer experiences and about particular organizations with which they're familiar.

6. TAKE CARE OF SOME TASKS EARLY ON.

Use the first few months to accomplish a few tasks that will ease the burden once you actually can contact employers. Such tasks include preparing or updating your resume, compiling a reference list in case employers require one, and preparing a generic cover letter that you can adapt to different employers.

7. KEEP AN OPEN MIND, AND CONSIDER MANY POSSIBILITIES.

While narrowing your focus will help make the job search easier, you can and should apply to as many jobs as suit your interests and needs. Keep in mind that the more applications submitted, the better your chances are of landing a job. If in doubt, it never hurts to inquire about a job and apply if interested.

8. KEEP PERSPECTIVE.

Don't panic if you feel the first semester is quickly passing by and you do not have a job. You are not expected to begin your search until the end of the semester, and all first-years are in the same position. Employers know that and do not expect to hear from first-years until December.

Like anything else in life, try to approach the job search in a relaxed manner. You will find something; it may just take some time.

9. BE CREATIVE.

There are so many opportunities out there. While this is an important summer for many of you to gain your first legal experience, be flexible in your job search and go after your dreams.

10. Don't be heartbroken if you can't find legal work in your first summer.

Believe it or not, this first summer is not the most important in terms of the job search. The vast majority of students get the best jobs in their second summer. Some of you may not find legal work the first time around. Don't be disappointed. You have another summer ahead.

The rest of this chapter is designed to give you specific tips and outline pros and cons about various opportunities you may want to consider. Since the vast majority of students usually pursue public interest or firm jobs, these will be the primary focus, with other types of opportunities discussed at the end.

Public Interest Work

I went to law school with the intention of doing public interest work. Hence, once the first term of law school was finally over, I was eager and excited to talk to potential employers. Since all my plans centered on public interest work, I immediately pulled out Harvard's public interest employer guide. On one of the first pages, I noticed the address for the American Civil Liberties Union of Alabama. As soon as my eye caught this announcement, I decided that that was where I wanted to work. After a phone interview with the legal director of the ACLU of Alabama, I was hired (primarily due to the fact that Yale has an excellent summer funding program for students doing public interest work).

My experience at ACLU of Alabama was absolutely incredible—in part because I was the only full-summer law clerk for the ACLU and in part because I developed a wonderful working relationship with my supervisor, the one attorney in the office. Unlike some of my classmates who went to work for law firms or large public interest organizations, I was expected to assume all the work of an ordinary lawyer with the ACLU rather than that of an intern. It was very demanding and very fulfilling. From day one at the ACLU of Alabama, I was thrown headfirst into a major litigation plan. For several years the ACLU of Alabama had been researching the issue of First Amendment violations in the public schools; it was time to bring a "school prayer" case—and that was my job. I realized that I had so much to learn and so quickly (so much that you learn in law school has no immediately apparent applicability to the litigation process). For example, one of my first projects was to develop and coordinate our plaintiff class and assist in the drafting of a class action complaint. I certainly did not learn how to do these tasks in my first-year curriculum (which, as an aside, leads me to emphasize the importance of participating in a law school clinical program if one is offered, so that you have the opportunity to gain some practical experience). Project after project unrolled rapidly, and each one was more exciting than the next. I worked 50 to 60 hours per week—solely because I wanted to, not because my supervisor expected or instructed me to. Each new project gave me the opportunity to learn not only more about the law, but even more importantly, more about how to litigate. After completing my internship, I felt as though my legal knowledge had been increased by at least 100 percent. In fact, for the next two years, I would always joke that the only place I learned the law was at the ACLU of Alabama. As such, I highly recommend that every law school student who is even remotely interested in the field to spend at least one summer doing public interest work.

My second summer was split between the ACLU of Alabama and the Criminal Defense Division of the Legal Aid Society of New York. I returned to Alabama primarily because I felt such a deep commitment to the work that I had been doing there and because I felt as though I had work to complete with the lawsuit that had been filed partly as a result of my work the prior summer. In fact, to this day, I still track the Alabama lawsuits that I worked on while I was there (and my supervisor still keeps in touch with me, constantly reminding me of his appreciation for the work that I did at ACLU of Alabama). I think that sentiments such as these in some sense describe the beauty of public interest work. For the most part, public interest organizations are understaffed organizations, full of hard-working, down-to-earth, smart people, that are always looking for dedicated individuals to help with their work. I am not sure that my friends who worked for law firms their first or second summers had the same warm feeling about their employers or places of employment that I had about ACLU.

—Jody Yetzer, Yale Law School

Many students pursue public interest opportunities during their first summer and find the work very rewarding. The jobs seem to be more plentiful for first-years, yet funding seems to be more limited.

You may be asking exactly what does "public interest" work mean. It's what the name says: you can serve various segments of the public, whether through individual representation, impact litigation, or other avenues, such as policy work. Public interest jobs are ideal for those who have a passion for serving others, who are deeply concerned about issues of social importance, who want client contact, and who have an independent source of funding or for whom funding is not a major issue.

TIPS TO KEEP IN MIND WHEN SEARCHING FOR A PUBLIC INTEREST JOB

1. SOLICIT ADVICE FROM SEVERAL SOURCES.

When deciding where to apply, talk to other students, consult with career counselors, read student reviews from past years as well as public interest guidebooks, and try to get a sense of which organizations would be the best fit for you and would most suit your interests. Also, there are several public interest job fairs that you should consider attending as a way to network and make contact with a broad range of employers. Sometimes attendance at these fairs can lead directly to an offer.

2. SEND OUT LOTS OF RESUMES AND COVER LETTERS, AND BE ENTHUSIASTIC.

Should you decide that you want to pursue public interest work, be prepared to send out many cover letters and resumes. Adapt your cover letters and resume to highlight your relevant experiences. Even if you have had no experience in an organization's practice area, don't be shy. Just be sure to show your enthusiasm for public interest work and the basis for your interest. Indicate in your cover letter whether you have an independent source of funding; public interest organizations will generally welcome you with open arms if you come with your own funding. Also, indicate whether and when you would be available for an office interview or phone interview. Remember, though, to keep cover letters short and concise; no matter how interesting you think it is, employers don't have time to read your whole life story.

3. REMEMBER THAT PATIENCE IS A VIRTUE.

A final but important point to keep in mind as you apply for public interest jobs: Don't be discouraged if you don't hear from public interest organizations right away. Many organizations are understaffed and overburdened, and they may not respond as efficiently as you were hoping to the flood of applicants they receive each year. Be patient, but also be persistent. Follow-up phone calls appropriately timed usually cannot hurt. Don't give up on organizations just because you have not heard from them. Better to call than to make any assumptions about their interest in you—chances are, they haven't seen your resume yet; a phone call for the purpose of inquiring about the status of your application can bring it to their attention. And, if you will be in a particular city where you applied for jobs around the holiday time or thereafter, be sure to let them know that you will be available for an in-person interview or an office visit.

> *I came to law school after spending two years teaching in an urban public school system. Entering law school, my goal was to become a children's advocate. Come December of my first year, I applied to at least a dozen organizations around the country specializing in representing children. I landed the ideal job at a wonderful office in San Francisco—Legal Services for Children—that exclusively represents children in such matters as abuse, neglect, guardianship, and special education cases. I enjoyed every minute of my summer internship. My tasks were varied: legal research and writing, client interviews, home visits, courtroom preparation, and screening intake calls. What I remember most about the summer, however, were the people—both the lawyers and social workers who worked in the*

office and the clients whom they represented. The attorneys and social workers were some of the most dedicated and competent people I had ever met, and several served as wonderful mentors to me. The contact with the child clients and their families was constant, whether by in-person visits or by phone, and this was undoubtedly the most rewarding aspect of the job. The clients had very immediate needs, and they appreciated our efforts on their behalf. The smiles on their faces when we stopped by for a visit at their foster home or their expressions of gratitude when we helped them achieve their objectives made the job so worthwhile. Throughout the summer, I saw firsthand how a lawyer could help a child navigate his or her way through the legal system and bring some order to the chaos in their lives. Enjoying the work as much as I did also confirmed for me—at a time of doubt—that there was at least one area of the law by which I truly felt inspired.

—Deborah Koven, Yale Law School

PROS AND CONS OF PUBLIC INTEREST WORK

Pros:

- You will be helping people in need, so it's the kind of work you can feel really good about.

- Countless opportunities exist to pursue the area of the law that most interests you, whether it's advocating on behalf of homeless people, immigrants, domestic violence victims, abused children, prisoners, migrant farm workers, or criminal defendants; the list goes on and on.

- You will have lots of client contact and "human" interaction.

- There are opportunities to work on important impact litigation cases that can affect the lives of many people or to represent individual clients and to advocate on their behalf.

- Opportunities exist to work with diverse clientele and potentially to use foreign language skills.

- You will work with some of the most interesting, bright, enthusiastic, creative, and dedicated attorneys you will ever meet—attorneys who are usually motivated more by the cause they represent than money.

- The potential exists for a lot of responsibility, especially since many of the organizations have limited resources and welcome the assistance of summer interns. You may find yourself handling many aspects of a case, conducting client interviews, drafting legal documents, and helping to develop legal strategies.

- This work presents excellent training opportunities with respect to advocacy skills, legal writing, and legal analysis.

- You will have opportunities to observe courtroom proceedings, appear in court under attorney supervision, and help represent clients in administrative hearings.

- You will have opportunities for networking with other talented people in the field.

- Generally speaking, the hours will be more manageable than firm jobs.

- At last, you will have that once in a lifetime opportunity to impact the life of someone less advantaged. You may not be able to save the world, but you can try to help solve some very real and important problems.

Cons:

- Funding may be limited. Many public interest offices welcome volunteers or pay only a minimal salary. You may be required to find independent sources of funding (check with your school about school funding/fellowships) or to forgo a salary in exchange for an interesting legal experience.

- While limited resources mean that you will get to do more as an intern, it also means that you may not have access to some resources, such as a full-service law library, online computer services, and office personnel. You may have to be creative in finding resources or learn to work without them.

- The recruiting/application process can be slow and inefficient and may require an extra degree of patience and persistence on your part. You must be proactive in finding opportunities—they will not necessarily come to you.

- Because most public interest organizations do not know what their needs or funding will be in the future, it is unlikely that a summer internship will lead to an immediate offer for permanent employment or even a future offer.

- The work may not be as glamorous as that with a firm. No free lunches or Broadway shows.

LAW FIRMS

The first-year summer job search is gruesome, particularly if you want to work at a firm. I sent out roughly 70 to 80 letters, mostly to New York law firms; 25 letters went to firms in Washington, D.C., and two letters went to firms in my hometown of Columbus, Ohio. As a result of those letters, I managed to get four interviews: two in New York, one in D.C., and one in Columbus. I also started to do on-campus interviewing, but fortunately before those interviews were complete, I received an offer from one of the New York firms where I interviewed. The firm that offered me a summer position was the New York branch of a large Chicago firm. There were approximately 35 lawyers. It turned out to be a great summer. I had a strong desire to work at a firm my first summer—preferably a New York firm—because I knew that ultimately that is what I wanted to do when I graduated, and I did not want my second summer at a firm (arguably the most important summer) to be my first time in such an environment. However, my brief story should make it clear that getting a firm job after your first year in law school is no walk in the park. Such is the case no matter what law school you attend. I would suggest that if you have your heart set on working at a firm the first summer out of law school, you should pursue that goal, but also be sure to investigate other options, such as working in the public defender office or externing for a judge. The obvious drawback of these jobs is the lack of pay, but they no doubt will provide needed writing and legal analysis skills. Plus, they are a gold star on your resume.

—Charlita Mays, Yale Law School

I spent the summer after my first year of law school working as a foreign trainee for a Japanese law firm in Tokyo. The experience was a memorable one, and I would encourage anyone interested in a transnational legal career to seek out a summer position abroad with a foreign firm. Learning how laws are made, applied, and interpreted in another country provides a valuable perspective on our own legal system. Exposure to an alternative legal regime made me realize, in a very tangible way, that there is never a single approach to any legal question. I believe this experience helped make me a more creative legal thinker and thus a more effective legal practitioner. In addition, I was involved in several interesting international transactions, and I made contacts with Japanese lawyers that I hope will prove useful in my future career. These advantages, along with the obvious appeal of spending a summer abroad, made for a very exciting and positive experience. I have no regrets about my decision to take a road somewhat less traveled. I found it a very enjoyable one.

—DARRELL HALL, COLUMBIA LAW SCHOOL

Many students also choose to work in law firms during their first summer. This experience can also provide excellent legal training. Generally, the salaries for summer associates far surpass those paid by public interest organizations, which is an attractive feature of law firm life, especially for those with heavy law school and college debts. If you are interested in applying to a law firm, there may be two routes to pursue. Some law schools sponsor an on-campus interview week for first-years, where several law firms come to campus and conduct applicant interviews. However, many firms do not come to on-campus interviews and therefore require you to take the initiative and submit a cover letter and resume on your own. Find out whether your school has an on-campus interview week and, if so, when it is being held. Inquire as to what firms will be coming. Research those firms as well as firms that will not be participating in on-campus interviews (probably the vast majority). Consider whether you want to apply to a large, mid-size, or boutique firm, or a combination of these; whether you want a firm that specializes in a particular area or one that has a more general practice; whether you want to work in the main office or a branch office; whether you prefer to be one among many summer associates or whether you are looking for a small summer associate program; and whether you prefer a place that represents mostly plaintiffs or defendants.

In deciding where to apply, keep in mind that many firms do not hire first-year summer associates or hire only a select few. Don't be discouraged. Many students will send a mass mailing of cover letters, resumes, and transcripts to upwards of 100 firms. From that bunch, they may be lucky to get one or two interviews. Again, if you really want to work at a firm, apply to many and be flexible as to location. Check ahead of time to see which firms hire first-years; do not waste your time or energy applying to firms that reserve their summer associate program solely for second-years. Your time will come soon enough.

> **TIP:** Some firms, including some of the most prestigious ones, hire minority students in their first summer as part of various recruiting programs. If you are a minority student, ask your career center about these programs and take advantage of them if you are interested in firm work.

PROS AND CONS OF WORKING AT A LAW FIRM

Pros:

- Opportunities exist for excellent legal training, particularly legal research and writing.

- Resources are plentiful. You will probably have access to a secretary, a copy center staff, a library staff, and so on.

- You will have opportunities to work with bright and accomplished lawyers.

- The great salary helps minimize debt.

- You will have high-profile clients and cases.

- There will be opportunities to experience several areas of the law, including litigation, corporate, trusts and estates, tax, and real estate.

- Travel is possible, including assignments to foreign offices.

- You can engage in pro bono work.

- There are free lunches and lots of summer social events.

- You may get an offer for permanent employment at the end of the summer.

- Law firm jobs are generally prestigious and look good on your resume.

Cons:

- It's very difficult to get a job the first year; many of the top firms won't even look at your resume.

- There are fewer opportunities for client contact.

- You may be given less responsibility; it is unlikely that you will be handling cases on your own or appearing in court.

- It is unlikely that you will be able to see a case through from start to finish; you'll just be there for a piece of it.

- You may be expected to work long hours.

- With all the wining and dining, you may not get a realistic perspective of what life is really like as a full-time associate.

CLERKSHIPS

I interned for a federal judge after my first year. It was a great job. The training, exposure, and interest level was fantastic. On the downside, the money ($0) is tough to get by on. An additional point that some people might not realize is that you can make excellent contacts. I have kept in touch with the judge and remained good friends with his clerks. The clerks, in particular, have been a wonderful source of knowledge about all the things of interest to a law student/young lawyer (e.g., firms, clerkships, other things to do with your J.D.).

The non-legal highlight of the job occurred one evening after work when the five interns and three clerks went out for a drink at a trendy bar. One of the clerks invited the judge, but no one really expected him to show. To our great surprise and delight, the judge did show up, bought everyone a round of tequila, and did a shot with us before leaving for the night.

—NOAH PERLMAN, COLUMBIA UNIVERSITY

Many students seek internships with judges after their first year of law school, and they report having very rewarding experiences.

Again, as with the other positions described above, research the judges carefully and, if you can, talk with others who have worked with that judge. Since you will be working in close quarters, it is important that you find a chambers with the right fit.

Pros:

- You will receive excellent legal research and writing training.

- You may find in the judge and other clerks wonderful mentors.

- There is opportunity for courtroom exposure.

- It's great legal experience, especially for those interested in litigation.

Cons:

- There's little to no pay.

- If you are the type of person who prefers to work in a large office with a lot of people, you may need to adjust to the close quarters of a judge's chambers.

- You may miss the experience of advocating directly on behalf of clients.

OTHER EMPLOYMENT OPPORTUNITIES

Although this chapter has focused on firms and public interest work, there are many other opportunities that students pursue. These will be listed below, not as an exhaustive list, but just to spark some ideas.

Also, remember as you begin your job search that not every student will be lucky enough to get his or her first-choice job. Some will not even get their last choice. Because the number of students attending law school has increased dramatically over the past few years, the marketplace for jobs has grown very competitive and tight. This fact is not intended to alarm you, but it is intended as a reminder that you must be thorough and creative in your search and be flexible in your decision-making process. Don't give up or get discouraged if things don't work out after you send the first wave of letters. Keep trying. Timing can be critical, as the story below demonstrates.

> *I decided to study abroad in Argentina after my first year because I felt that after that summer, I would not have much choice but to work. However, after I returned from Argentina, about six weeks of summer still remained. Immediately after I returned from studying abroad, I checked into available job listings at the career services office of the law school. There were four or five attorneys in need of research assistance, so I faxed my resume and a cover letter to all of them, and 24 hours later, I had a job doing research for a small firm and helping them prepare a trial exhibit for the fall. It was good experience because instead of a structured clerkship, the firm was so short-handed they threw me right into the research or exhibit preparation without much supervision. This allowed me to learn about legal practice in a more pragmatic sense than I had been able to during my first year of law school. Even after I started back to school in the fall, the firm still called me to do small research projects. After my first year in law school, I was fortunate enough not only to study abroad, but also to gain some valuable work experience. The combination of the two refreshed me for my second year, and both have been extremely valuable in my second-year clerkship interviews.*
>
> —Suzanne E. Schreiber, University of Tulsa Law School

EXAMPLES OF OTHER OPPORTUNITIES

- Study abroad program (many law schools have summer programs for which you can get academic credit)
- Research assistant for a professor
- Field work, such as human rights work abroad
- Legislative/policy work
- Paralegal at a law firm
- Management consulting or investment banking
- Working as an in-house counsel for a corporation

SECOND SUMMER

By the second summer, you'll be a pro at the job search, and hopefully you'll have one summer's worth of experience to add to your resume. The second summer job search varies from the first. Though the same opportunities present themselves, the process differs.

For those interested in working at law firms, most law schools conduct an extensive on-campus interview period. Before you leave campus at the end of your first year, make sure you find out when all resumes must be submitted for this process—usually this happens sometime over the summer. Be timely in complying with your law school's procedures, as you do not want to miss out on an interview just because your resume was mailed too late. Also, if you do not get an interview—as slots are limited—take the initiative to contact firms on your own and send your resume to these firms directly.

Some public interest and government organizations also participate in on-campus interviews, but the pickings are much more lean. If you desire one of those jobs, again, be proactive in contacting several employers, but this time around, you can do so right away rather than waiting until December. Also, consider applying for various grants in order to get funding, as most of these jobs are just as limited in terms of funding for second-years as they are for first-years.

Even more so than the first summer, the second summer may be a time to start thinking about where you want to work after graduation. If there is a place that you know gives preference to those who have summered there, and that happens to be a place that interests you, take a serious look and try to land the summer job. Most firms give almost all second-year summer workers full-time offers; full-time offers are slightly less plentiful in public interest and other types of summer legal work.

CONCLUSION

Your first summer job can be very rewarding, especially if you take the time up front to find the right type of job for you. Do your research, look for a good fit, weigh heavily your particular interests within the law, and choose wisely. Look upon your two summers as precious opportunities to explore the legal profession, gain practical legal experience, network, and start narrowing your focus as to what you want to do after graduating from law school. Hopefully you will feel as one student reported feeling after her two summers: she wished that she had "a thousand more summers to explore all the exciting and diverse opportunities that the legal profession has to offer!"

CHAPTER 11

Interviewing

"Well, this is it. I'm about to go into my first interview! And this firm is my first choice, too. Looks like my resume worked. Okay, now, concentrate. Look confident. Look professional. Look at my hands! Why are they shaking? I don't believe this. What time is it? At least I remembered to wear a watch. It can't be long now. I hope my knocking on the door a few minutes ago wasn't too loud. All I heard was a muffled 'One minute, please.' Did the interviewer sound aggravated? God, why am I so nervous? This is ridiculous! I've been through worse than this, a lot worse. It's no big deal—no need to panic, just relax. Deep breath . . . deep breath . . . good. Now, focus. Be calm, be cool, be collec . . . " CLICK! The door suddenly opens, the other student exits, you walk up to the interviewer (who seems nicer than you imagined), you extend your hand, and you say, "Good morning, I'm. . . . "

THE INTERVIEW

Every year, thousands of law students across the country interview for a limited number of summer associate positions, public interest internships, judicial clerkships, and permanent job offers. All of your work to reach this point—the endless reading, the copious note-taking, the exhaustive outlining—ultimately boils down to a professional outfit, a firm handshake, and 30 minutes of "casual conversation." Sounds a bit arbitrary, doesn't it? Well, arbitrary or not, the fact remains that no single event in your law school experience will have a greater impact on the shape of your career

than the nerve-wracking gauntlet known as the legal interview. But despite all that is riding on it (and don't be fooled, there is an awful lot riding on it), a legal interview does not have to be a nightmare. Just know what you're getting into, and be prepared.

> *The Three-Ls at your school will all tell you to "be yourself," "have fun with it," "be confident," and "imagine the interviewer in his underwear." (I would not recommend the latter if, like Georgetown, your school's on-campus interviews are held in hotel bedrooms. It begins to feel a little seedy.)*
>
> *However, what the Three-Ls might not tell you is that perhaps the most effective interview strategy is the same one that was vital to getting you into law school in the first place. Specifically, have the numbers they are looking for. Your fun, confident self will shine if you don't need to fabricate bumbling excuses for a low GPA.*
>
> —KEN ITRATO, GEORGETOWN UNIVERSITY LAW CENTER

TYPES OF INTERVIEWS

Interviewing for legal employment typically includes two stages: the on-campus interview and the callback. Although this chapter generally focuses on interviewing with law firms, most of these tips apply equally well to government and public interest jobs. This chapter also focuses mostly on second-year interviews because they are more extensive than first-year interviews. But, again, all the tips will apply equally well to first-years. First-year students, however, may not have callback interviews (in other words, a public interest group or law firm may decide your fate after only one meeting); in that case, first impressions may be all-important.

The On-Campus Interview

The on-campus interview is an initial screening process where the law firm, government agency, or public interest organization determines whether you meet its minimum hiring criteria. After reviewing your resume along with hundreds of others, the prospective employer will invite a select group of students to meet for 20 to 30 minutes with one of its lawyers. As the name implies, the on-campus interview usually takes place somewhere on-campus, though some employers use a local hotel as a venue. (For some reason, the phrase "at-a-local-hotel interview" never quite caught on.) Sometimes several law schools will organize an off-campus screening interview "fair" for law firms in distant states. At out-of-state career "fairs," screening interviews also often are held in hotels.

Although held under less-than-ideal conditions, the on-campus interview is a critical hurdle. Because of the limited time and the large number of students each interviewer sees (sometimes up to 20 a day!), it is imperative that you stand out from the pack in a positive way. This is, after all, the only first impression the employer will have of you. In a short amount of time, you need to "argue your case," which basically means communicating your ability to do difficult work involving complex analysis. Since this is a screening interview, be prepared to address the "threshold issues" of grades, class rank, law review membership, and so on, as these are more likely to come up here than during the callback. If you have some 'splainin' to do, now is the time to do it. It is this first impression, along with the strength of your resume, that will determine whether you will get invited to interview at the prospective employer's place of business.

Interviewing at the Offices of a Prospective Employer

Hopefully, your performance during the on-campus interview will be rewarded with an invitation to participate in a callback interview.

Your credentials are satisfactory and you have passed the initial screening interview—now you will spend the better part of a day at the place of business of the prospective employer, interacting with several people who may be your future colleagues and coworkers. The callback is where you really need to shine, where the rubber meets the road, where they separate the . . . well, you get the point.

The purpose of the callback is to engage in a mutual process of selection, to see whether there is a good fit between you and the prospective employer, which will predict future success. Notice the word "mutual" in the preceding sentence. Although the tendency is to focus on the prospective employer's judgment of you, it's important to remember that the callback is a two-way street. A truly successful interview (yes, there is such a thing) should also allow you to piece together an overall profile of the firm's practice and culture, and to explore your potential role within it.

What exactly happens during the callback? Though each employer follows its own formula, in most cases you will go through a series of 30-minute one-on-one interviews with four to five different lawyers. Each interviewer then makes an independent judgment on your candidacy, which is factored into the hiring committee's decision whether to offer you a position. Sometimes, the callback will also include either lunch or dinner at a local restaurant with you and two to three lawyers. (By the way, if they stiff you with the dinner check, it is *not* a good sign.)

Sometimes you will have an initial interview at the offices of a prospective employer. This is especially true of small firms, government agencies, public interest organizations, and firms that do not recruit at your law school. Your experience at such an interview will be similar to the above description. However, it will also be your chance to make a good first impression. Usually, during an initial in-office interview, you will meet with one or two attorneys. If you interview well, you will probably be invited back to meet more attorneys.

INTERVIEWING TIPS

1. KNOW WHAT THEY'RE BITING ON.

If you want to catch fish, the first thing you need to ask is "What are the fish biting on?" In the same way, give some thought as to what motivates the firm to go through the time-consuming and expensive interview process. Obviously, a good law firm needs to hire people who will be successful lawyers, people who are *able* to do the work well, who are *motivated* to do the work well, and who will *work well with others* in the firm. Fortunately or not, your fact-filled resume has only limited value in identifying whether you are such a person. The firm also wants to know whether you possess those intangible personal qualities that are not necessarily reflected in your resume but are nevertheless required of a successful lawyer.

What are these intangible personal qualities? From the moment you walk through the door to the moment you leave, the interviewer will wonder: "Will this person be able to forge the kinds of relationships with clients and colleagues that are necessary to a successful practice?" "Will this person inspire confidence in others?" "Does this person convey the measure of poise, maturity, and self-assurance expected of a lawyer?" "Is this person assertive but not abrasive, an attentive listener, with a degree of tact and good humor that puts others at ease?" "Will I want to work with this person?" Keep these things in mind while we consider some ways that you can help the interviewer answer these questions in your favor.

A public interest employer will want to know that you have a sincere interest in the substantive area of law to which it is devoted. For example, if you interview with the Children's Defense Fund, highlight your past experience working with children or for children's causes.

> *Occasionally you hear stories about interviewers who ask really off-the-wall questions meant to rattle the interviewee—for instance, requesting that the student explain the meaning of collateral estoppel. But most interviewers are just interested in determining whether you're the kind of person they'd enjoy working with—do you have a sense of humor, are you generally pleasant and engaging, or are you an arrogant bore? So the best thing you can do in an interview is to try to enjoy it and reveal some of your personality (unless, of course, you have the kind of personality that should be kept under wraps!).*
>
> —COATES LEAR, UNIVERSITY OF VIRGINIA SCHOOL OF LAW

2. DO YOUR HOMEWORK.

You will hear this advice ad nauseum, but preparation really is the key to a successful interview, as it is in every other part of your law school experience. Before you walk through the door, you should learn everything you can about the firm, something about the lawyers with whom you will be meeting, and enough about yourself to know which things to emphasize and which to "explain."

Gathering information about the law firm—its practice, reputation, and philosophy—is absolutely fundamental to preparing for your interview. You should check with your law school's career services office and ask for copies of the firm's brochure, access to the Martindale-Hubble law firm directory, and other sources of basic information. Don't forget to make use of the online resources available to you; visit the firm's Web page, or run a search of recent newspaper articles mentioning the firm in one of the "free" legal databases. *The Insider's Guide to Law Firms* is a remarkable resource for "inside information" on a select number of big firms in the larger cities; if those are the types of jobs you are interested in, you should buy a copy. Finally, it's always helpful to talk to your classmates who have interviewed at the firm and to professors who might have an opinion of the firm and its practice.

Knowing some basic information about your interviewer can also be useful. Call the firm's legal recruiter a day or two before the interview to get the names of the lawyers with whom you will be meeting. Look them up in Martindale-Hubble; chances are, you went to the same college as one of them. Ask who is on the hiring committee and what practice areas they are in; this might help you tailor your interview appropriately. Knowing whether a particular lawyer is a partner or an associate can also be instructive, since associates tend to be a bit more forthcoming about quality of life issues. That said, do yourself a favor and resist the temptation to "impress" anyone with your detailed knowledge of the interviewer's alma mater (unless it is the same as your own), publication history, bar association membership, hometown, and other personal data. With very rare exception, dropping such information during an interview is less impressive to the interviewer than it is disquieting. Remember, you're interviewing for a job as a lawyer, not as a stalker. No successful interview ever included the remark, "As a Libra, you'll probably agree that my resume is well-balanced."

Learning about yourself, at least in the context of preparing for an interview, includes an awareness of the strengths of your candidacy for a job in this firm. One good exercise is to write out your best answers to commonly asked questions, and practice ways of delivering these succinctly and with enthusiasm. Take the time to participate in videotaped practice interviews or workshops offered by your career services office. Review your senior thesis, job history, extracurricular activities—*everything* mentioned in your resume is fair game for the interviewer. And pay special attention to your writing sample; it has a surprisingly powerful influence on the deliberations of the hiring committee, sometimes even to the point of counteracting the negative (or positive!) effect of your grades or class rank.

3. SCHEDULE YOUR CALLBACKS EARLY.

If at all possible, schedule your callback appointment immediately after receiving an invitation to do so. (Just one caveat: If you have a favorite firm, consider doing a "warm-up" interview with a less desirable firm first.) On one level at least, the hiring cycle is nothing more than a numbers game, with each firm extending its offers on a rolling basis. It's preferable, then, that the firm make a judgment on your candidacy *before* it has made offers to many other candidates. Think of it like being in a parade of elephants—it's better to be at the head of the line than near the rear. Some firms and other legal organizations will only hire one first-year, so being up front can be a big advantage (noting, of course, that first-year interviewing does not begin until December).

While on the phone scheduling your callback, let the legal recruiter know if you're interested in a specific practice area, since they may be able to tailor your callback accordingly. Also, if you live in another city, clearly establish which travel and lodging expenses the firm will cover. And, lastly, do everyone a favor and immediately decline any invitations to firms that no longer interest you; sitting on a useless offer does you no good and might just kill another candidate's chance for his or her dream job.

4. ARRIVE EARLY AND LOOK TO SEE WHETHER THERE IS A "FIT."

On the day of your callback, bring an extra copy of your writing sample, resume, and transcript (even if you have sent these already). You should arrive at the firm about 15 minutes ahead of your appointment (being late is not an option), at which time you will most likely be greeted by the legal recruiter, who will provide you with a copy of the day's itinerary. Glance down the list of names and note any last-minute changes in interviewers. The legal recruiter will then walk you to the office of the first lawyer with whom you will be interviewing.

As you walk through the firm's hallways, take note of the more subtle cues of the working environment. Do people seem to enjoy working together? Do they show signs of respect for one another? Is the atmosphere pleasant and professional? Remember, the firm is on stage here too, and these cues can sometimes make all the difference if you later find yourself in the enviable position of deciding between multiple offers.

5. Be respectful.

During your interview, how you act is as important as what you say. Your demeanor should try to establish a relaxed, businesslike rapport between you and the interviewer. Offering a firm handshake, smiling while introducing yourself, sitting up straight, and maintaining good eye contact are essential here, though not entirely sufficient. Instead of a cross-examination, your interview should be a pleasant, flowing conversation between two engaging people. Make it as easy as possible for this person to take 30 minutes out of a busy workday to interview you.

How do you do this? The easiest way to develop positive rapport is by finding a common area of interest or experience between yourself and the interviewer. Be sensitive to your surroundings. When you enter the lawyer's office and take your seat, glance at the walls and bookshelves. See if you can pick out something in all that mess that you can use to establish a personal connection and enliven what otherwise might be just another mind-numbing interview. "Oh, I see you fly-fish" will put a smile on the face of even the most distracted interviewer (assuming, of course, that there is some evidence that the interviewer actually fly-fishes!). Keep the focus on your qualifications by drawing connections between the interviewer and things in your resume (last summer's job, undergraduate experience, and so on). Appropriate body language is important, too; keeping respectful eye contact, modulating your voice, nodding in agreement, or flashing a genuine smile all show a level of engagement with your surroundings. Listen carefully when the interviewer is speaking, and follow up with an appropriate question or comment. This will go a long way to *show* that you and the firm are a good fit.

You will hear an awful lot of advice about "being yourself." There are two classic miscalculations to approaching an interview: Some people feel the need to project a false image of themselves according to what they think the interviewer wants to see, while others have a "here I am, take-it-or-leave-it" attitude. There is a world of difference between showing yourself in the best light possible on the one hand and being misleading or downright deceptive on the other. Deception fools no one and is unethical and ultimately disastrous. "Being yourself," however, is not inconsistent with framing the conversation in the light most favorable to your candidacy. Definitely be yourself, but be yourself *at your best.*

Be prepared for anything, and be able to think on your feet. During one callback, the chair of the hiring committee asked me two questions. The first was about affirmative action programs at the firm and what I as a Latina thought. The second question was what I thought about Saddam Hussein. As to the first question, I had thought about the issue on my own, but I was a little hesitant to talk forcefully about it at an interview. However, since he asked, I answered honestly, and, more importantly, I backed up my opinion with logical arguments. As for Saddam, I think his point was to test how articulate I was—whether I could make an argument on my feet.

Don't act surprised at anything that comes up. Take a breath, think about what you know, and then answer the question honestly. Being calm, articulate, and confident is essential to a good interview (as well as showing your personality!). By the way, I got an offer from that firm.

—NANCY SERRANO, NEW YORK UNIVERSITY LAW SCHOOL

6. BE CONFIDENT, BUT NOT COCKY.

While it's perfectly natural for your first few interviews to feel pretty intimidating, don't let that keep you from speaking freely about yourself and your accomplishments. Recognize your Achilles' heel beforehand, and turn that sow's ear into a silk purse so you avoid crying over spilt milk under the bridge (winner: most mixed metaphors in a single sentence). If a difficult issue comes up, don't apologize or sidestep it. Answer the question, and then move on to greener pastures. There is a good reason why the firm is using otherwise billable time to interview you. Take advantage of this opportunity by making the most compelling case possible for yourself. This is not to imply that boasting is a good idea, though (after all, the student coming in after you is a Rhodes scholar). Just realize that when interviewing for legal employment, modesty is a greater sin than pride.

7. ASK NOT WHAT THE FIRM CAN DO FOR YOU . . .

An easy way to score points during the interview, and to break a dreaded silent pause, is to ask an appropriate question about the firm or about the interviewer's practice. Your preparation should include developing a list of thoughtful open-ended questions ("What, why, how, tell me about . . . "), and you should choose two or three that are appropriate for each particular interview. Some commonly asked questions are "What kind of feedback should I expect?" "What is the firm's training program like?" and (my favorite) "What do you like most about practicing at X, Y, & Z?" Pay close attention to the flow of the conversation, and avoid questions that repeat issues already discussed.

The callback is not the appropriate time to scrutinize the firm's policies regarding family and maternity leave, benefits, vacations, profit distribution, and minimum billable hours. In addition to the risk that you will be misinterpreted, focusing on these issues wastes precious interview time and diverts attention from your qualifications to your requirements. Wait until *after* you get an offer before addressing these important questions with someone at the firm. Or find your answers by referencing firm data on file in the career services office of your law school. A successful interview does not begin by strolling into a partner's office and saying, "Hi, a pleasure to meet you, does your insurance cover dental?"

8. PREPARE FOR THE INEVITABLE QUESTIONS.

If there is one certainty you can prepare for in life (death and taxes being outside the purview of this book), it is the inevitable litany of questions you will face during your interview. Most of these questions are fairly predictable: "What interesting project did you work on last summer?" "Tell me about your involvement in moot court?" "What brings you to firm X, Y, & Z?" "What other firms are you considering?" and "What do you expect to like least about practicing law?" (Single worst answer: "Working with blood-sucking lawyers like yourself.") Play it smart and prepare clear and concise answers to these questions *before* arriving at the interview. Granted, every now and then you will get an unanticipated question, but such curveballs should come as infrequently as possible. When they do, be flexible and craft your answer so as to emphasize your qualifications for the job. Whether expected or not, deliver your response in such a way that avoids any hint that you are giving yet another canned answer.

> *As soon as I heard his office door click shut behind me, a heavy silence fell over the room. His questions were slow in coming and lent themselves to one-word answers: "How are you liking your second year?" "Did you have trouble finding our office?"*
>
> *I guessed that he was not accustomed to interviewing, or maybe he was shy, or maybe just tired from all the work that was scattered over every visible surface. But I also figured that his assessment of me was going to be a factor in whether I got an offer, and at that moment, things*

looked dim. Clearly, what this interview needed was an interviewer. Clearly, it wasn't going to be him. That left me.

I started out genuinely enough, asking him how he came to be at the firm and what drew him to the city. That pretty easily slid into questions about what area he practiced in and what kind of work was strewn about the room. Everyone—even dud interviewers—is interested in themselves, and he was no exception.

The conversation began to flow more easily, and, as I feigned interest in his practice area, he even began to show glimmers of enthusiasm. Scintillating it was not, but it was better than sitting there in silence for the requisite 30 minutes—or worse, hearing myself repeat the answers I'd given to every other interviewer who asked the stock questions.

As he walked me through the hallway to the next interview, he continued chatting like we were good friends. I was reasonably confident that this was an interview that he, at least, thought had gone well and that such a sentiment would be reflected in his recommendation to the hiring committee. Big smile and handshake at the end; it was very nice to meet him.

—Alix Biel, Yale Law School

9. Tell a story.

When preparing for some of the more predictable questions, think of some good stories that you might tell that relate an answer in a more interesting way. For example, if the interviewer asks you why you went to law school, don't just say, "I always wanted to go to law school." Tell a story, such as "When I was in college, our sorority got in some legal trouble for having sponsored a party with alcohol . . . " or "I want to be a lawyer because I don't want to be in a position like my grandfather . . . " or "My favorite character in L.A. Law was the tax lawyer because. . . . " Be sincere. Be interesting. Be funny (but not corny). A few canned stories (that don't seem canned, of course) will liven up the interview proceedings. Try out the stories on a significant other, family member, or friend. If they think the story is no good, your interviewer is probably going to be even harsher.

10. REMEMBER THAT DISCRETION IS THE BETTER PART OF EVERYTHING.

We are all about to enter a profession whose very existence depends on the discretion of its practitioners. The style and content of your interview should reflect an ability to observe the written and unwritten rules of the profession. Show good judgment when discussing your prior work experience by keeping confidential the names of clients you worked with last summer. If you are a first-year, keep confidential the names of clients you may have worked for as a paralegal or in some other job during or after college. Never criticize a former employer or colleague—your interviewer will rightly wonder, "Will we be next?" Be particularly sensitive to any biases (i.e., sexism) that can creep into your vocabulary. While at dinner, order tonic water or iced tea—save the alcohol until after the interview (when you might really need it). Assume nothing. Well-placed, appropriate humor can be one of the most effective ways to establish a comfortable rapport with your interviewer, but use your best judgment. Strike a balance that is neither earnest nor silly. No matter how relaxed things are or how friendly people seem to be, never risk alienating your interviewer by using sarcasm or risqué language. No one wants the next round of jokes to include "Did you hear the one about the student who blew the big interview with an inappropriate comment?"

11. Remember the "E" word.

Remember when you were a kid and you would ask an adult why there is a Mother's Day and a Father's Day, but no Children's Day? The answer would inevitably be "*Every* day is Children's Day." Well, in the same way, ask any firm what it looks for in a candidate, and you will get the same answer: ENTHUSIASM. Evidence to the contrary notwithstanding, public interest groups and law firms want to hire people who are exciting, interesting, and even (believe it or not) fun! Show some spark in your interview; talk about something that really interests you, some passion you have. Who knows, your interviewers may share a similar passion (or feel so envious that you have a life that they *have* to hire you). Be positive about your candidacy, and avoid like the plague anything that will give the interview even a remotely negative feel. Again, don't bad-mouth *anything*, especially your law school, classmates, and past employment.

On the topic of enthusiasm, don't leave the room without having expressed your strong desire to work for *this* firm. As unbelievable as it sounds, lawyers have egos too, and they appreciate knowing that their firm is your first choice. Demonstrating a strong desire to work at this firm is particularly important if you are interviewing in a city to which you have no obvious ties. As always, support your assertion with concrete facts. Noting that your spouse or partner has ties to the city is much more convincing than something like "You know, I've always wanted to live in Toledo."

12. Keep Going . . . and Going . . . and Going

Simply put, the callback is exhausting. It is basically a long, grueling day of being at your absolute best. Get a good night's sleep, and keep the adrenaline going. Remind yourself that the last person with whom you interview is as important as the first.

13. Leverage other offers.

Leveraging other offers is a risky, but potentially lucrative, strategy. Law firms and certain public interest groups are very competitive with one another. If a firm knows you have an offer at one of its major competitors, you can be assured that the firm will take a second and third look at your qualifications. Leveraging other offers does not mean outright bragging or mentioning your other offers to every lawyer who interviews you. Subtle hints to one or two lawyers will do the trick. For example, one of your questions might be: "I have an offer at X competitor. How would you compare the two firms?"

Leveraging can backfire if not used wisely. You cannot and should not leverage offers from firms that do not compete with the firm you are considering—in fact, some lawyers are so egotistical that they will be offended that you would even mention the other firm in the same breath. You cannot and should not leverage an offer from a firm in another city. Talking about interest in another city will open up a Pandora's box that is better left closed.

14. WRITE THANK-YOU NOTES IMMEDIATELY.

Immediately after your callback is over, you should write a personalized, businesslike thank-you letter to the firm. Some students send individualized letters to every lawyer at the firm or public interest group. Such a time-consuming tactic may not be worthwhile for every firm or organization. Another option is to send one letter to the hiring partner and make note of the other people with whom you met. Send your letter right away, since firms usually make offers within a few days of your callback. If for some reason you feel motivated to phone one of your interviewers, send flowers or candy, or drop by to thank them in person, please take a moment to lock yourself into a closet until this urge completely passes. Instead, do something productive and make good notes of the day's events. Hopefully, you will receive offers for employment from several firms, and your notes will prove indispensable as you consider which offer to accept.

CONCLUSION

Interviewing for legal employment, while difficult and time-consuming, can reap incredible rewards. While years of hard work can be undone by a poor interview performance, a well-prepared, honest, and enthusiastic interview can help you land the job of your dreams. Good luck!

—by Paul G. Sweeney

CHAPTER 12

Adjusting to Daily Life: The Psychology of Surviving Law School

By now, some of the elements of novelty have worn off. You're registered; you've made it through the introductory week, met some classmates, tested the social climate at the first day reception, and had some casual conversations. You've now met your professors and had some first glimpses at their subject matter. Hopefully, you're all settled in your personal quarters and you've located the local grocery and sampled at least a few of the city's nicer aspects. You're "here" and a bit more "settled." It's nice to have you.

But there's still newness about the whole experience and a lot of powerful feelings not too far under the surface—some special kinds of joys and some special aches. A bit of the initial thrill is still there. There's a longing for the sight of some familiar places, and especially some beloved faces. New beginnings always invoke wondering: "How will I fit into this group?" "How will I do here?" "Will I really like it in the long run?" Uncertainty is as inevitable as it is discomforting. There is the excitement of a new challenge and the deep joy of having the dreams of going to law school realized at last. There is some apprehension about the hours of study and the publicized difficulty of the courses. The test scores of the class are at very high levels, so you can be confident. But this is also the competition! Certainly there's an element of pride in having been admitted to a first-class law school—as in all of the other achievements which made admission possible. Yet being an achiever is something of a burden. It's a bit relentless. Past performances have to be kept up, and this is a faster league. Can't let down hopes of family, friends, one's people—not to mention one's own hopes. All these swirling feelings are entirely normal and even commendable up to a point. But not when they cause undue anxiety. It may help to know there ARE lots of "feelings" floating around the first few weeks and months of law school. They involve everybody in your class, so don't feel alone and perhaps try to laugh about them with each other.

—FATHER JAMES B. MALLEY, S.J., PROFESSOR, BOSTON
COLLEGE LAW SCHOOL

SOME STRESS IS INEVITABLE

No matter how laid-back you are, law school inevitably brings out many emotions. Unlike college, where you have a year or two to settle in and figure out the system, academic success in the first year of law school can be outcome-determinative (see Chapter 10, "The Summer Job Search," on finding a job). The pressure, whether self-imposed or external, causes, at the very least, moments of meltdown.

One common misconception about law school is that law students are stressed out all the time. Despite brief periods of sheer lunacy, most of the day-to-day aspects of preparing for class are not that stressful. If you pace yourself, you'll be surprised at how manageable and enjoyable law school can be—at least most of the time. Nevertheless, even the most disciplined students experience days or weeks when the workload seems unbearable or the law seems incomprehensible. These times can bring about stress and anxiety. Stress is most easily recognized by its symptoms—the emotions that accompany it.

YOU'LL KNOW YOU'RE STRESSED IF YOU FEEL . . .

Angry

You may harbor hostility during your first year. It is common to feel anger toward professors. "Why won't they just spell it out? Why do we have to go through this crazy Socratic torture dubbed 'the case method.' I can learn to think like a lawyer without it. Why is the professor assigning so much reading? I hate the professor. The professor is stupid. The professor does not deserve to be teaching at this school."

You may also get angry, annoyed, and perturbed at the significant others (for example, your husband or wife) in your life because they don't understand, because they complain that you are not spending enough time with them, and because they are normal human beings (and you are not anymore).

Confused

In law school, you learn a problem-solving approach. This is what law professors like to call "learning to think like a lawyer." Most professors believe that the best way for students to learn this problem-solving approach is by "hiding the ball." What this means is that professors ask many difficult questions and never give the answers. Sometimes professors do this because they want you to figure out the answer on your own. Most of the time professors do this because there is no "right" answer.

Many first-year students come to school thinking they will learn rules (formally called blackletter law). It soon becomes apparent that the rules are not pivotal. What is important is not clear. The Socratic Method can feel like an attempt to make over your personality. What you learn your second year is that it is—sort of. You will be amazed to realize how differently, and more clearly and critically, you think as a result of suffering through the Socratic Method your first year. You may even appreciate it. However, during the first few months of your first year, you will probably not recognize the changes in your thinking, and the Socratic Method will leave you confused.

Anxious

First-year students are well acquainted with anxiety. Anxiety over whether you are "getting it" as fast as the competition. Anxiety over whether law school was the right decision. Anxiety over grades and career choices.

You may have a tendency to catastrophize: "I'm going to flunk this Bankruptcy exam and then I'll never get a job and then I'll never pay off my loans and I'll have to declare bankruptcy—but I don't understand bankruptcy, which is why I'm going to flunk this exam." Resist this type of thinking. It will do you no good and may give you an ulcer (ouch!).

> *I read* One-L *before going to law school and thought Scott Turow was completely neurotic. I promised myself not to stress out the way he had.*
>
> *During finals of my first year, I picked up the book again. As I reread certain passages, I smiled in recognition. Suddenly I realized that I was Scott Turow. I was horrified at what I had let myself become.*
>
> —Shannon Gottesman, Boston College Law School

Lonely

You may be attending law school in a new city far away from familiar faces. There are times when it would be great to grab coffee or shoot hoops with someone who truly knows you. Even if you are attending law school in your hometown, old friends don't always understand what you are going through or have the patience to put up with your "law school" problems.

You will make new friends at law school who are in your boat, but there is a tendency to hide what you are really feeling—your true emotions—from new friends. You may not trust them yet. You may not want to reveal your weaknesses.

Depressed

Life is the pits. You're tired. You're not having fun anymore.

SOLUTIONS: STOP THE MADNESS

Talk Things Out

All the emotions mentioned above are common and normal during your first year. Talking with others about what you are going through helps keep things in perspective. Drop by the dean of students' office and share your concerns—you'll be reassured. Talk with a professor about your anxiety over a class. Who knows, the professor who assures your sniveling self that it "all will make sense in time for the exam—stay fluid" may be the same person who goes to bat for you your second year so you can get that great federal clerkship.

Most importantly, don't forget to talk things out with classmates. You'll probably get a great laugh and be surprised when your friends admit they are dreaming about torts, too.

Keep a Sense of Humor

Laugh. At yourself. At your professors. At classmates (behind their backs, of course). Laughing is a great stress release.

Find a sectionmate with a good sense of humor who likes to make jokes at your and others' expense and try to spend as much time as possible with that person.

Keep Perspective

As mentioned previously, some stress is normal during law school. You will make it through. You will pass. You will get a job. This, too, shall pass.

Get Some Sleep, and Don't Forget to Eat

There is enough work in law school that a person could conceivably not sleep during the week—or at least only sleep a few hours a night. If you are the type of student who feels compelled to do the supplemental reading, overcome that urge if it cuts severely into your beauty rest.

Similarly, if you are the type of person who forgets to eat during times of extreme stress, make sure to remind yourself to EAT! You really will think better if your body is fueled.

Pray

If you practice a particular kind of religion, take time to attend religious services. Services will give you time to relax and remember the big picture. If you do not enjoy religious services, but still believe in something bigger than yourself, pray on your own.

When the Stress You Feel Is Not Normal

Sometimes the stress of law school rises to a level where you need more than a few laughs to make you better. If you feel many of the above emotions constantly or for more than a few days, you may need professional guidance. Here are some signs of severe stress that may be unhealthy:

Tense muscles

Headaches

Constant colds

Sexual dysfunction

Severe insomnia

Rapid breathing

Sweating

Loss of appetite

Diarrhea

Trembling

Withdrawal from personal relationships

Uncontrollable crying

Feeling empty

Excessive use of alcohol, uppers, cola, coffee, tobacco, or pot in order to feel normal

Compulsive cleaning and organizing

We all experience some of the above occasionally, but if several of the signs begin to show up and do not go away, you should talk to your dean of students, doctor, or someone else you trust about getting more help.

If you see one of your friends becoming severely depressed, make sure you talk to him or her and even recommend that he or she seek help. If that person resists help, and you are truly worried, talk to the dean of students or other appropriate person at the law school. Do not try to solve problems that are over your head. Unfortunately, some law school students commit suicide every year. Risk losing a friendship if the consequences are truly dire.

POSITIVE ASPECTS OF DAILY LIFE

Believe it or not, many lawyers remember law school as one of the best times of their lives. The flexibility of the student lifestyle is especially appreciated by people who had careers before coming back to law school.

YOU WILL MEET INTERESTING PEOPLE

Your classmates will be from diverse backgrounds, religions, and countries. Many students will have special ties from former careers that will add to your learning. Almost everybody you meet will be intelligent and motivated.

LAW SCHOOL EXPOSES STUDENTS TO MANY SUBSTANTIVE AREAS

To understand law, you have to understand the subjects that the law governs. For example, to understand real property law, you must have a general understanding of deeds and mortgages. Similarly, to understand income tax, you must understand annuities and dividends—or at least know what they are. Most professors teach students about the substantive areas that the law in their classes covers. Thus, you will gain a broad understanding of many areas:

Health Law → Medicine

Tax, Corporations, and Emerging Enterprises → Business and Accounting

Negotiation and Criminal Law → Psychology and Sociology

Constitutional Law → History

Intellectual Property and Cyber Law → Technology

FLEXIBILITY

As a law student, you will have the flexibility to spend time doing the things you enjoy because you can study whenever you want. You can exercise in the middle of the day, spend a few hours volunteering or watching television, or go to the movies. You are working for yourself.

LAW SCHOOL IS INTELLECTUALLY RIGOROUS

Law courses are challenging intellectually. You will probably find that you are pushed beyond your academic comfort zone—possibly for the first time in your life.

Professors and classmates will challenge your assumptions. You will learn new critical-thinking skills.

A NOTE TO SIGNIFICANT OTHERS

Those of you who care about someone starting law school probably have many questions and apprehensions of your own. This section will briefly address some common concerns you may have.

WILL HER OR HIS PERSONALITY CHANGE?

Any experience in life changes us in some way. The most common complaint about law students is that they become more argumentative or strident. Although saying law school changes a person's personality is a generalization, it is true to some extent. Law students become very comfortable debating issues and unconsciously may try to debate every aspect of their personal life as well as tort policy.

You probably will also get tired of hearing about the law and recaps of the cases your significant other finds amusing.

> *My mother decided rather late in life that she wanted to be an attorney. As I entered high school in California, she was starting Harvard Law School in Massachusetts. At spring break, I flew to Massachusetts, and we drove her car together back to the West Coast. With exams approaching, she brought along her legal texts and read as I drove.*

She would read a case, sigh, and then complain for a while about how boring the law was. Eventually, she brightened. "Look, it's not all boring. Here's a negligence case about a flour mill. The holding—which is where the court gives its opinion—says, 'we hold it self-evident that persons in charge of flour barrels should not drop them out of windows.' Funny, huh?" Hysterical.

A few years later, my wife started law school at Boston University. My wife is a far more cheerful person, and she came bounding through the door after her first day of Torts class with an amusing anecdote to share with me. "Listen to this," she said, "the professor told us this really funny story about a flour mill today."

When I finally started law school at NYU, five years after my mom graduated and during my wife's third year at Boston University, I was looking forward, if not to nonstop entertainment, at least to new stories. New York, I figured, is a long way from Boston, and surely the professors will have different stories to share. My first class was Torts, and the professor dutifully cautioned us that we would have to wade through a lot of really dense legal writing over the next three years. However, she assured us, even judges have a sense of humor. "Let me share my favorite holding with you," she offered.

Yep, it was about a flour barrel, and, yep, it was probably the only interesting story of the year.

—Keith Scully, New York University Law School

WILL I EVER SEE HER OR HIM?

Although the law school curriculum is challenging and demanding, you will probably see your significant other more than you think. The beauty of being a student is the flexibility of hours and the ability to always work at home.

What may be affected is the quality of time spent with your significant other. Much time, especially the first year, must be spent studying. In addition, your law student may be crabby or irritable for reasons unknown to you.

The good news is that much of this goes away the second year. Second- and third-year students work hard, but they are used to the routine and less stressed. In addition, because first-year grades are the most important for finding "coveted" big firm jobs, the pressure academically is greatly reduced after the first year.

WHAT CAN I DO TO MAKE THE NEXT THREE YEARS PALATABLE?

The best thing to do is develop a life of your own. Focus on your own career and pick up old hobbies or find new ones. Make friends to socialize with apart from your significant other.

You should also remember to keep your sense of humor. Feel free to make light of your significant other's neurosis. Try to make your law student laugh, too.

Finally, remember that law school will be over in three years. After law school graduation, you will have the pleasure of the bar, 2,000 billable hours per year, and important trials that eat up weekend after weekend.

WHAT TO DO IF YOU HAVE CHILDREN

> *More than anything, going to law school while bringing up two children alone has been a logistical challenge. I found myself scheduling my courses around my children's school and activity schedules and around baby-sitters' schedules. No matter how carefully I planned, however, I often found myself bringing a child to class or to the library with me, or getting paged in the middle of class when carefully worked-out logistics fell through or a child was ill.*
>
> —ANONYMOUS, BOSTON COLLEGE LAW SCHOOL

If you have children, you will be faced with an even more difficult challenge. You may find yourself in the minority, but there is help and support. Most law schools have social groups for families. The groups get together for holidays, play-dates, and basic support.

You should also stop by and introduce yourself to the dean of students. That way, if an emergency with your child comes up, the dean will already understand your situation. The dean also has the power to reschedule exams and possibly tape classes for you if problems arise.

If you have school-age children and school is canceled or child care falls through occasionally, most professors understand if you bring your kids to class. You may be able to use the day care on the main campus of the undergraduate school with which your law school is associated.

—by Shannon Gottesman

CHAPTER 13

Having a Social Life at Law School

YES, YOU CAN!

Success in law school and a satisfying social life need not be mutually exclusive. But this isn't college, and making a social life for yourself will require more effort for several reasons. For instance, your law school class will probably be a lot smaller than your college class. Students also probably live more spread out from one another than they did in your undergraduate school. Many of your law school classmates will be married, engaged, or living with a significant other. In addition, you will have more schoolwork than you did in college, and the other students will be more stressed out than your classmates in college. But don't lose hope; there are other fun-loving future lawyers out there who don't just want to spend the next three years languishing in the library.

The key to a balanced life at law school—which includes both work and play—is time management: that is, making time for yourself to have fun and still get your work done.

Here are some suggestions to help clear your schedule for some very necessary fun. But underlying all of these tips, remember that if you were a fun person before you came to law school, that does not have to change. Seek out others with the same priorities you have, and let the festivities begin!

TOP 10 TIPS TO KEEP YOUR SOCIAL LIFE SCINTILLATING

1. DON'T REINVENT THE WHEEL.

You are not the first person to take Civil Procedure. Your law school bookstore is brimming with commercially prepared outlines and other study aids (see "Andy's Picks" in Chapter 3, "Preparing for Exams," for suggestions on the best commercial study aids). Although these products are not substitutes for the real thing, they provide a basic layer of knowledge that will save you time and energy. In addition, former law school students who took your classes with your professors will often "pass down" outlines that they themselves have made. In some cases, these outlines are virtual transcriptions of your professors' lectures and reading assignments. Commercial and student-made outlines will save you time by clarifying your reading assignments and perhaps obviating your need to create an outline of your own.

> *Listen to what second- and third-year law students—as well as recent graduates—tell you about classes, studying, jobs, and professors. They know what they are talking about, because they have been through it, and what you learn from them will save you time and help you relax.*
>
> —JESSICA POLLOCK, GEORGE WASHINGTON UNIVERSITY LAW SCHOOL

2. FIND A STUDY BUDDY.

Studying for finals can be a lonely (and long) period. Do not attempt to do it alone. There is no need for an intense, full-fledged "study group" straight out of Scott Turow's

One-L (remember the scene with the resumes?), but a study partner (or perhaps two or three) is a great idea. Find another student in your section who seems concerned about doing well, but who also is a fun person with social tendencies. Not only will studying in a pair (or perhaps in a small group) improve your grades through discussion and shared materials, but it will make you feel less like a prisoner. Balance your studying with short breaks (like a snowball fight or a coffee/junk food run), and sometimes treat yourselves to a real reward—like a whole two-hour movie. Your study partner will also be a great source of moral support at the most stressful period of your first year.

> *My first year, we had finals after New Year's, so we had about two and a half weeks between our last class and our first final. My friend, Monica, and I both decided to stay in New York over the break, and since we were in the same section, we decided to study together for our exams. We settled on a system of coffee shops and movies. Every day for those two and a half weeks, we would find a different coffee shop at which to study. We would spend about six or seven hours pounding lattes and arguing tort theories and other useless concepts. After we were sufficiently wired and sick of studying, we would find something completely non-law related to do. We would either go out to dinner, go see a movie, or go hang out at a bar with the few others who decided to spend the weeks in New York. All in all, it was a good way to keep sane during a very stressful and scary period in our law school career.*
>
> *—RONEN ELAD, COLUMBIA LAW SCHOOL*

3. Don't worry about what other people are doing.

There will always be law students with color-coded outlines, sophisticated charts and graphs, and insightful classroom comments on the first day of school. Ignore these people. First, one of the little-known facts of law school is that those who talk the most in the class do not get higher grades than students who quietly take notes and never participate. Second, people talk about doing work much more than they actually do it. Third, time spent worrying about what others are doing is time that you are not productive and time that you are not relaxing and having fun.

> *Try to remember that the people who say they are going to stay home and study on Friday or Saturday night probably will not get any work done, so you might as well go out and have fun instead of sitting at home watching TV alone.*
>
> —Michelle Zinman, George Washington University Law School

4. Know when to turn it on.

There are two very good reasons to go out on the town during the law school year: December and April. In those months, your social life will have to take a hiatus because of exams. Resist the temptation to let finals "season" start four weeks into the semester, because you will be unable to maintain your pace. Making time for fun—whether it is going to a bar, the movies, or dinner with friends—will help you stay focused later, when it really counts.

5. Have non-law school friends.

Stay in touch with friends from high school, college, or work who are not in law school. Friends who live near your law school, but are not involved with the law, are particularly important for your social life, because they will remind you that there is a life outside

Torts and Property. When things look grim, and you need to get away from it all, give one of these friends a call.

6. GO TO ORGANIZED SOCIAL EVENTS.

Most law schools organize social events for students. Don't pass these opportunities up just because they might remind you of your junior high school dance in the school gym. Many students attend these functions, particularly during orientation week or on special occasions like Halloween or Valentine's Day. Some schools even organize a formal or semi-formal event during the year. If you attend these functions, you will see that a lot of other students are out having fun, not home studying. Attending school social events early on will help you identify which of your classmates are willing to work hard at having fun, and then you can make your own social plans with that group outside the school setting.

7. KEEP YOUR NIGHTS FREE.

Law students often have long blocks of time between their classes. Use this time to your advantage. Make a habit of setting this time aside to do the next day's reading assignments. This should make a large dent in the amount of work you have to do in the evening, and it might even free up your evening and nighttime hours completely.

> *My first year, my school set up our schedule so that we had hours between our classes on a given day. It was easy to sit out in the sun and waste that time, but it made more sense to just go to the library and get the next day's work out of the way. So when we left school that afternoon, we were free until the next morning. At night, it was like we were not even in law school, because we could do whatever we felt like doing.*
>
> —RACHEL GOLDENBERG, UNIVERSITY OF FLORIDA LAW SCHOOL

8. BE A LEADER.

Don't just wait around for fun to spontaneously take place around you. At some schools, this just will not happen. So be a leader, and inspire others to take the first step away from their books by tempting them with something better. Make an announcement at your Friday class that a group of students will be meeting at a local bar for happy hour. Organize a party in your dorm, or invite people over to your apartment. Get a group together to attend the opening night of a much-hyped action movie. If you give your fellow students a reason to leave the library, they will.

> *Near the end of my first year, a group of my friends and I began a tradition that has continued until the present. Every Monday night at about 10 P.M., we all meet at a local bar to hang out, play pool, and drink. It has gotten to the point that you need a hell of an excuse to miss a Monday night—even a final the next day won't cut it. We have grown to such a large group, sometimes reaching 50, that we tend to almost take over the bar. This has become a great way to let off steam and hang out in a non-law school context.*
>
> —RONEN ELAD, COLUMBIA LAW SCHOOL

9. GET INVOLVED IN EXTRACURRICULAR ACTIVITIES.

You can improve your social relations even without leaving the law school campus. Most schools have extracurricular activities to suit students of every conceivable interest (see Chapter 6, "Law Reviews and Journals," and Chapter 7, "Extracurricular Activities and Moot Court"). There are journals, political groups, and advocacy clinics that provide law students with great legal experience and spontaneous fun. Even law students will loosen up when put into a large enough group. And these groups often organize social events for their members.

Meeting people through activities can also help you academically, because second- and third-year students involved in the groups will have outlines and advice that will help save you time, thereby giving you even more time to do what you want.

10. Get off campus and explore.

> *I bought a set of tapes on Federal Income Tax. My friend and I got in the car and drove to Walden Pond, then up to New Hampshire, listening and learning about tax law. We stopped for dinner in a small town, and we did some sightseeing on the way back. It was a great way to study without being trapped in the library, and it's a time my friend and I will always remember.*
>
> —Shelly Hirschtritt, Harvard Law School

Get away! If you or a friend have access to a car, take a road trip to see the local sights or to go visit a friend. Or buy a guidebook to the area in which your law school is located to find out what public transportation will take you into the "real world" (even if it might just be a half an hour away). Go skiing or learn to snowboard in the winter. In the spring, take an early trip to the beach. For students living in the big city, a trip to a suburban shopping mall or multiplex movie theater might be enough to give you the distance you need to remember that you had a social life before you came to law school, and that you still can, too.

—by Sarah Kotler

CHAPTER 14

Living Arrangements

THE RIGHT ROOMMATE

Your living arrangements will have a big impact on your law school experience. Roommates who understand the pressures of the first year can be great support. But gaining perspective from a roommate who works in another field can also help maintain sanity.

Think of your studying style when considering your housing options. Will watching peers study create stress? If your 9-to-5 roommates go to happy hour after work, will you be able to resist? Could you put up with your mother to save a bundle on expenses by living at home? A living arrangement that lets you balance studying with a social life (see the previous chapter, "Having a Social Life at Law School") is crucial to law school survival.

FACTORS TO CONSIDER WHEN CHOOSING LIVING ARRANGEMENTS

> *I wanted a school that guaranteed housing for at least the first year. I didn't know any potential roommates and dreaded looking for an apartment back East when I was living in Seattle.*
>
> —MELISSA MORGAN, NEW YORK UNIVERSITY LAW SCHOOL

ASK IF ON-CAMPUS HOUSING IS AVAILABLE

Find out if on-campus housing is even an option. Some schools, especially those in cities, don't offer housing for law school students. If your school has dormitories, ask the housing office the following series of questions:

- Do students share rooms? Can you get a single room?

  TIP: When deciding whether to share a room or live alone, balance the extra monetary cost of going solo against privacy concerns.

- Is the building secure?
- Do the apartments have kitchens?
- Is there a meal plan?
- Are there accommodations for married students?
- Are utilities included?
- What percentage of students live on-campus?
- And, most importantly, do you share your bathroom with just your roommate or with everyone (plus the cockroaches on the seventh floor)?

Having been out of school and living independently for three years, I approached a return to university housing with no small trepidation and dread. Make no pretenses, university apartments are merely glorified dorms in terms of the physical space (small rooms, dorm-issue furniture) and temperament (the gossip mill, pizza parties). It did take time to adjust to certain aspects of communal living—working out bathroom time and sharing kitchen space, not to mention dealing with

> *"different" personalities! It may seem trite, but the upside of the experience outweighs any negative aspects. I've made the best friends I think I will ever have. The bonds you form as a One-L are made that much stronger when you pull an all-nighter with your roommate or go to the gym at midnight to blow off some steam. It becomes obvious to you that only those who have gone through the law school experience can understand what you are dealing with; why not surround yourself with those same people?*
>
> —LAURIE CHURCHILL, NEW YORK UNIVERSITY LAW SCHOOL

ASSESS YOUR LONG-TERM HOUSING GOALS

Once you determine that you could live in campus housing, assess your long-term goals. Ask if your school guarantees housing all three years. If you are planning to practice in the city where your school is located, you might want to invest in a house or apartment right from the start.

However, remember that most on-campus housing is subsidized by the school and may be a good place to start. If you are planning to spend your summer in another city, on-campus housing is sometimes the best option since you only pay rent during the school year and don't have to worry about subletting your apartment to a stranger.

> *When I moved into my apartment, I had a roommate who was very congenial. At first, it looked like the beginning of a budding friendship. However, I quickly discovered that she was overly*

> *aware of her contributions to the apartment. For instance, if she felt she had made the requisite purchases of toilet paper, she would hide the remainder in her room. She kept a mental table of every contribution. If she felt someone else should clean the bathroom, she would never think to do it herself.*
>
> *Although things were fine on the surface, there were underlying tensions. The moral is tit-for-tat makes no friends.*
>
> —ALLISON STEINER, NEW YORK UNIVERSITY LAW SCHOOL

REMEMBER THAT YOU ARE NOT LIVING IN A FRATERNITY/SORORITY HOUSE ANYMORE

Law students come in all shapes, sizes, ages, and backgrounds. Many don't enroll straight from college, so expect that your roommate might have a life outside of school. Your roommate may not be looking for more drinking buddies, so observe basic rules of courtesy to prevent roommate tension. Keep the volume down on your stereo, and make sure your 15 fun-loving friends leave by midnight.

Don't expect an immaculate room simply because you're in professional school. The roommate who spends two hours briefing a case might not spend two minutes making her bed. However, this is law school, and you can get a jump start on your mediation class by negotiating early with your roommate over issues such as noise, cleaning, and the phone bill.

PLAN SOME TIME AWAY FROM YOUR ROOMMATE

The first year is like rabies; sooner or later, everyone will go a bit crazy. Your objective is to stay calm and unaffected by your roommate's paranoia. First-year roommates can be a great source of support. They are going through the same experience at the same time. And swapping horror stories about cold-calling reminds you that you're not the only one who thought that a brief was just a fashion statement by Calvin Klein.

Trust yourself. You made it through college; you know how to study. If your roommate panics because it's October and he hasn't begun to outline, say something comforting, then get some space. It's easy to assume that your roommate has a better idea of what to do. The truth is, he's as clueless as every other first-year.

> *Where do I begin? My roommate, a Three-L, has rubbed off on me in a bad way. We'll go to movies, we'll go out, we'll find any excuse to procrastinate—we even went to a high school football game 40 miles away. He hasn't gone to any of his classes; there was one class where he had a paper due, but he didn't know if it was due on Monday or Thursday. The moral: Find a roommate who goes to school; you'll get a lot more done that way. Don't move in with a roommate who is absolutely brilliant and never needs to study at all.*
>
> —Jason Olson, University of California at Berkeley (Boalt)

GET PERSPECTIVE FROM A SECOND- OR THIRD-YEAR ROOMMATE

If your roommate is a second- or third-year, you will have the benefit of his perspective, his experience, and his outlines! These students are more relaxed than the first-years, and they will remind you that it is possible to do well without briefing every single case.

But remember that much of their attitude is rooted in confidence. After all, they survived. Chances are, you won't achieve their brand of hubris until you live through the experience yourself.

GET OUT OF THE DORMS DURING FINALS

> *After my Contracts exam, I was horrified to hear students discussing the answers in the dorm elevators. When plugging my ears and humming didn't drown out the sound, I got out and walked up the 10 flights. It was the only time I absolutely hated living in the dorms.*
>
> —MELISSA MORGAN, NEW YORK UNIVERSITY LAW SCHOOL

During finals, living on-campus can be a blessing. There are people around at any hour to discuss First Amendment rights and due process.

During finals, living on-campus can be a curse. You'll eat, sleep, and breathe law in December, and you'll need a break from the dorms, even if it means studying at the Starbucks down the block. Listening to students discuss exam answers by the mailboxes or in the dining hall can be painful to your psyche and confidence. Take breaks. Read *People* magazine. Catch a Jackie Chan flick. And remember that there is a world outside the dorms and the law library.

THINK ABOUT LIVING AT HOME

If you can stomach your mom's meat loaf and neatness directives, consider living at home. The price is right. You'll have more space. You'll have clean clothes. And your parents aren't likely to discuss Civil Procedure over dinner.

Discuss boundaries with your parents if you choose to live at home. Explain the pressures of the first year. You are not in high school, and the days of curfew are gone, but you are living in their house and must respect their lifestyle. Living at home might entail more family obligations but may offer an easy way to save on rent while pretending to laugh at Uncle Marty's jokes.

CONSIDER LIVING OFF-CAMPUS

> *The reason I decided to live with a friend from high school is because I figured I'd be in law school 24-7 studying. When I came home to relax and study, I didn't want a roommate who would be stressed out and talk only about law school classes. I wanted someone who would be my link to the real world.*
>
> *Living off-campus has been great for the most part, but occasionally there are problems. One time, I had a memorandum due at 8 A.M. on a Friday. Just my luck, there was a big accident on the Santa Monica Freeway, so I had to whip out my map and find an alternate route to get to school on time, which I did with time to spare.*
>
> —ALEX JACOBS, UNIVERSITY OF SOUTHERN CALIFORNIA LAW SCHOOL

When law school has completely consumed your life, it is the lucky student who can leave campus housing for an apartment where roommates aren't pondering the latest Supreme Court decision. Living off-campus may be a great way to maintain sanity, especially for students who have been out of college for a while. You can choose your neighborhood, cook your own food, and room with an aspiring actor, yoga instructor, sous chef, or a friend—whomever you choose.

> *Since I grew up in New York, I had an active social life with family and friends before law school that I wanted to keep up. That's why I chose to take an apartment off-campus when I enrolled in Fordham Law School. Living alone, you lose the campus feeling and you're not as much a part of the academic environment, but it helps to keep the stress level down and gets you out of the artificial campus environment where everyone around you talks only about school. When you can step away from the classroom, you can get a better perspective on your schoolwork.*
>
> —AARON RUBIN, FORDHAM LAW SCHOOL

If you live off-campus, you can treat law school as a job. You might stay at school from 9 A.M. to 6 P.M. and then have a real life outside of school in the evenings and on weekends. But before signing a lease, ask the following questions:

- How far is the commute to school?
- Is the area safe?
- Are utilities included?
- Is there a bus stop/subway nearby?
- Is there ample parking?
- How are the laundry facilities?
- What type of financial/time commitment is required?
- Can you sublet in the summer?
- Is there a decent pizza place nearby that stays open until 3 A.M.?

LIVE WITH FRIENDS WHO WORK TO STAY CONNECTED TO THE OUTSIDE WORLD

Your roommates may seem more supportive of you if you are not in competition with them for those four A's your Torts professor will grant this term. But remember that if you are living with friends in the working world, they may not understand your law-induced emotional peaks and valleys as well as fellow students. Those who live off-campus are not only geographically removed from school, but distanced from the school community as well.

REMEMBER THAT THERE IS NO PERFECT HOUSING SITUATION

As you choose your living arrangement, remember that even the best situation won't be perfect. Most lease and dorm commitments are only one year. You can always experiment with different options next year.

—by Melissa Morgan

CHAPTER 15

The Minority Experience

> *Yes, law school is tough and may present particular challenges for minority students. But if you rise to the occasion, it can be one of the most intellectually rewarding experiences of your life. Personally, I felt empowered by the analytical and advocacy skills I acquired in law school.*
>
> —MARTINA STEWART, HARVARD LAW SCHOOL

Law school is a difficult, challenging experience for all students. As with almost all other aspects of life, law school may present particular challenges for minority students. Therefore, what follows are some thoughts and advice for minority students as they approach law school. Before beginning, it is worth noting that there is no single "minority" experience in law school (or anywhere else). The goal of this chapter, then, is not to define a minority student's possible experience at law school. Rather, the chapter seeks to provide a list of issues for minority students to think about and perhaps to offer a few words of wisdom from those who have been there before. In this chapter, the term "minority" is used broadly to encompass women, students of color, students of different religions, and students who are gay, lesbian, or bisexual.

LIFE (AND PERSPECTIVES) INSIDE THE CLASSROOM

Despite decades of thought to the contrary, the law is now widely understood to be an inherently political and politically charged enterprise. Because the law has historically neglected and, oftentimes, engaged in outright discrimination against minority groups, minority law school students may often see the law's political nature as inherent and ever present.

This perspective on the law *and* on the process of being taught how to be lawyers often places minority students in a unique position during classroom discussions. For example, female students may object to the way in which their Criminal Law professor teaches the law of rape; gay, lesbian, and bisexual students may object to how their Family Law professor chooses to frame a discussion of marriage; African-American students may not agree with a Constitutional Law professor's stance on discrimination issues. At moments like these, minority students (especially during the first year) are often presented with the difficult choice of expressing an opinion that is likely to be controversial and inconsistent with existing legal traditions. Although some minority students may find these moments uncomfortable, the best course of action is always to speak up and state your views. Such moments are the first test of your ability as a lawyer to present a position and convince others of its persuasiveness.

MINORITY GROUP ACTIVITIES: KEY QUESTIONS TO CONSIDER

Most fair-sized law schools have activities and groups run by and for minority students. If you are a minority student, you probably will find yourself wondering early on if and how much you should become involved in minority student activities. Although the answer is different for each individual, here are some key questions to consider:

1. How important is it for you to feel part of a group?

The first year of law school can be a difficult, demanding time of adjustment academically, personally, and socially. Furthermore, despite the fact that law school has become much more "user-friendly" in the past couple of decades, it remains an isolating and alienating experience at times. Minority students, perhaps even more than other students, may feel alone or isolated, both inside and outside the classroom. Affiliation with a minority group may provide you with a sense of belonging and make adjusting to the first year a bit easier.

2. How much time are you willing and able to dedicate to minority activities?

Law school can be stressful, making some personal "down" time essential for your health and success. Therefore, you should carefully consider which extracurricular activities you want to participate in and how much time you are willing to devote. Chances are, you will want to participate in several law school activities, both minority and non-minority related. But belonging to several groups can be very time-consuming. You need to consider time constraints when planning your level of commitment. Don't overburden yourself, and don't neglect personal time to enjoy your favorite non-law-related activities or just to "veg" out.

3. What are the possible social/political implications of involvement, and how will you deal with them?

You should realize that group involvement may put you in some uncomfortable situations. For example, gay, lesbian, or bisexual students who become openly and heavily involved in the gay law students' association may be labeled "queer activists" because of this association. Although labeling of this sort should not discourage your involvement, it is something to think about before becoming involved. If you choose to respond to other students who question your reasons for participating in certain groups and activities, honesty is usually your best weapon. Tell them exactly why it is important for you to be involved.

LIST OF MINORITY GROUPS/ACTIVITIES

> *Harvard Law School has several organizations for those interested in getting in touch with individuals of Asian ethnicity. These include the Asia Law Society and APALSA (Asian Pacific American Law Students Association). The groups sponsor fun social events, big sib/little sib programs, community outreach, speakers, study tip sessions, interview and job search tips, and organizational meetings. The groups have gatherings with similar organizations at other graduate schools in the community as well. Your degree of involvement is up to you, be it largely social or politically active as well.*
>
> —LILY SO, HARVARD LAW SCHOOL

STUDENTS OF COLOR

- Student associations (for example, Black Law Students Association)
- Law reviews and journals focused on issues of ethnic identity (for example, *Latino Law Review*)
- Law-related and non-law-related community service projects that serve the local minority community

- Political action groups
- Clinical programs

WOMEN

- Student associations (for example, Women's Law Association, Women of Color Collective)
- Clinical programs focused on women's issues (for example, Domestic Violence Project)
- Law reviews and journals focused on women's issues, gender, and feminism (for example, *Women's Law Journal, Journal of Law and Feminism*)
- Law-related and non-law-related community service projects that serve women (for example, battered women's shelters and rape crisis hot lines)
- Political action groups

GAY, LESBIAN, AND BISEXUAL STUDENTS

- Student associations (for example, Lambda Law Students Association)
- Political action groups
- Law reviews and journals focused on issues of gender, sexuality, and gay rights (for example, *Journal of Law and Sexuality*)
- Clinical programs or volunteer opportunities relating to gay rights (for example, Lambda Legal Defense Fund)
- Social activities for members of the community

STUDENTS OF DIFFERENT RELIGIONS

- Religion-based student associations (for example, Jewish Law Students Association, Islamic Law Students Association)

- Law reviews and journals focused on law, religion, and morality (for example, *Journal of Law and Religion*)

- Political action groups

- Religious services

- Law-related and non-law-related community service projects that serve particular religious communities

SEEKING A BALANCE

Sometimes minority students feel both internal and external pressures to affiliate almost exclusively with their relevant minority community and, in the process, neglect connections with the mainstream, non-minority community. In the eyes of some in the minority community, a lack of total commitment is a sign of "selling out" or being ashamed of your heritage, background, or sexual identity. As a minority student, you need to start thinking about how much of a commitment you are willing to make and how you will deal with students who question your level of commitment.

Remember that you are not playing an all-or-nothing game. You can affiliate with your relevant minority community and not totally disconnect yourself from the larger mainstream community. In seeking a balance, you are likely to find a profound sense of belonging in the minority community, without losing the benefits of friends, organizations, and activities unrelated to your minority status.

DIFFERENCES WITHIN YOUR MINORITY COMMUNITY

Like any group, minority groups have their own tensions, differences, and divisions. Invariably, someone will fall into the minority, even in a minority group. For example, you may be a conservative in a traditionally liberal gay community or a feminist in a religious community that has always had conservative views about women's roles. There is nothing wrong with having different views, but you may want to think about how you will respond to others who question your beliefs. You may even inspire discussion within your minority community about some of these differences. Constructive (and sometimes heated) political and moral discussion is a definitive aspect of the law school experience both in- and outside minority groups.

MAKING AN ACADEMIC (AND PERHAPS A PROFESSIONAL) PURSUIT OUT OF YOUR MINORITY IDENTITY

> *I never took a set of courses in a defined area, but I did indulge my interests in things like Family Law, Gender and the Law, Constitutional Theory, Legal History, and Critical Legal Studies. Those courses were a nice counterpoint to more traditional courses like Tax, Evidence, and Corporations, which I also took.*
>
> —MARTINA STEWART, HARVARD LAW SCHOOL

Like most colleges, most law schools offer courses in minority studies (for example, Feminist Legal Theory, Gender and the Law,

Gay Legal Theory, and Race and the Law). Because of the usual absence of issues of race, gender, sexuality, and religion from traditional law school coursework, minority students may feel particularly drawn to these courses. Although "majoring" in minority legal studies during law school may not be possible, undertaking a planned, coherent, and comprehensive course of study in one or more minority legal fields is quite feasible.

If you decide to structure your law school studies with a focus on minority issues, you should consider complementing your interest in minority legal studies with a more traditional legal field. For example, just about all areas of minority legal studies are complementary to Constitutional Law and Theory, Legal History, Legal Theory, and Critical Legal Theory. Furthermore, to round out your studies, you should consider doing relevant clinical work and being involved in a journal or law review related to your interest in minority legal studies.

Although it may seem far off now, decisions about what you might do after law school must be made very soon after you begin your legal studies. One such decision for all students, and especially for minority students, is whether to pursue a legal career in nonprofit, public interest, or civil rights fields. For example, the struggle for black equality in America was precipitated by civil rights litigation in the 1950s. Today, some of the most interesting and effective work in the field of gay rights is occurring through impact litigation and legislative advocacy. Although this career path has its obvious negatives and positives, it is an option you ought to consider as you prepare for law school and being a member of the legal profession.

—by Martina Stewart

ABOUT THE AUTHORS

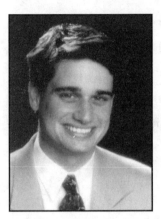

GREG GOTTESMAN

Undergraduate: Stanford University

Law School: Harvard Law School

Activities: Law Review, Movies, Chess, Golf, Tennis

Best Piece of Advice: "If you think you are talking too much in class, you probably are."

SHANNON GOTTESMAN

Undergraduate: University of Southern California/University of Washington

Law School: Boston College Law School

Activities: Movies, Holocaust and Human Rights Project, Student Coordinator of Note Taking Program for Disabled Students, Golf

Best Piece of Advice: "Take the night off before an exam. Go to a movie and relax."

CARTOONISTS

JUSTIN INGERSOLL

Undergraduate: Harvard University

Law School: Boston College Law School

Activities: Reading, Drawing Self

Best Piece of Advice: "Don't learn from experience if you don't have to."—Mama

MICHAEL McCORMACK

Undergraduate: University of Colorado

Law School: Boston College Law School

Activities: Cartooning, Chess, Woody Allen Movies

Best Piece of Advice: "Know thyself."— Oracle at Delphi ("And stock up on caffeine and Pop Tarts.")

CO-AUTHORS/CONTRIBUTORS

JOANNA GIORGIO

Undergraduate: Bucknell University

Law School: Boston College Law School

Activities: Note-taker for Disabled Students, Intern at Department of Interior, Solicitors Office, Teacher of Environmental Law at Boston College, Research Assistant

Best Piece of Advice: "Don't get caught up in the race for the pot of gold at the end of the rainbow. Everyone's pot of gold is different, and you could end up losing sight of the reason you decided to go into law school in the first place."

JODI GOLINSKY

Undergraduate: Brandeis University

Law School: Brooklyn Law School

Activities: Who has time for activities?

Best Piece of Advice: "Law school is stressful in and of itself. Do yourself a favor by rising above the competitiveness and pettiness and enjoying the intellectual experience. Participate in class and find your own voice."

TODD KIM

Undergraduate: Harvard University

Law School: Harvard Law School

Activities: Law Review, Drama Society, Research Assistant, Undergraduate Proctor, Writing, Music, Rollerblading

Best Piece of Advice: "The law school experience teeters wildly between the fascinating and the absurd. Make sure to preserve your intellectual curiosity and your sense of humor so that you can appreciate the one and survive the other."

DEBORAH KOVEN KLEIN

Undergraduate: Stanford University

Law School: Yale Law School

Activities: Student Director of Advocacy for Children and Parents Clinic, *Yale Journal of Law and Feminism*, Initiative for Public Interest Law, "I Have a Dream— New Haven" (Tutor in New Haven Schools)

Best Piece of Advice: "Get involved in clinical programs—the one place in law school where you can truly learn to practice law and be a skilled advocate."

Sarah B. Kotler

Undergraduate: University of Pennsylvania

Law School: Harvard Law School

Activities: Vacation

Best Piece of Advice: "What doesn't kill you makes you stronger."

Richard S. Lobel

Undergraduate: Stanford University

Law School: New York University Law School

Activities: Moot Court Board (Editor), International Law Society

Best Piece of Advice: "Try to strike a balance between work and play. You should be serious when you study but have some serious fun as well."

Melissa Morgan

Undergraduate: University of California, Berkeley

Law School: New York University Law School

Activities: Juggling, Tap Dance, Lacrosse, Riding Amtrak

Best Piece of Advice: "When all else fails, burst into song!"

Kimo Peluso

Undergraduate: University of California, San Diego

Law School: Harvard Law School

Activities: *Harvard Law Review*, Research Assistant

Best Piece of Advice: "Don't be afraid to let law school change you; you might actually like what you become."

Neal Potischman

Undergraduate: Swarthmore College

Law School: Harvard Law School

Activities: Intramural Basketball, Law Review

Best Piece of Advice: "The One-L year is like a marathon; don't work too hard in the first couple of months, and don't leave all your work until the night before finals. It's a long year, so pace yourself."

Dan Ralls

Undergraduate: University of California, Santa Barbara

Law School: Boston College Law School

Activities: Cinema History, Writing, Hiking

Best Piece of Advice: "It's only school. They're only exams. Relax."

Martina Stewart

Undergraduate: Yale University

Law School: Harvard Law School

Activities: Theater and Stage Management (college), *Harvard Civil Rights-Civil Liberties Law Review*, Teaching Assistant (law school)

Best Piece of Advice: "Follow your heart."

Paul G. Sweeney

Undergraduate: Saint Anselm College

Law School: Boston College Law School

Activities: Political History, Classic Jazz, In-Line Skating, Boating, Carpentry

Best Piece of Advice: "The first year of law school is a marathon, not a sprint. Develop a steady pace to your studies, and avoid burning out too early."

Jim Trilling

Undergraduate: Indiana University-Bloomington

Law School: Harvard Law School

Activities: Notes Editor, *Harvard Law Review*, Kids and the Courts Project, Tenant Advocacy Project, *Journal on Legislation*

Best Piece of Advice: "Enjoy law school!!! Expect it to be challenging and frustrating. It will be. However, it is also a very fun and interesting three years. Anticipate the challenges and the frustrations so that you have plenty of time to enjoy."